# JOHN WESLE

:

THE

# SUNDAY SERVICE

OF THE

# METHODISTS

IN

# NORTH AMERICA

with introduction, notes and commentary by

## James F. White

OSL PUBLICATIONS

Maryville, Tennessee

# JOHN WESLEY'S PRAYER BOOK:
## The Sunday Service of the Methodists in North America
### with introduction, notes and commentary by James F. White

Copyright © 1991 by James F. White
Second Printing 1995
Third Printing 2008

ISBN 978-1-878009-10-4

This book is printed on acid-free paper that meets the
American National Standards Institute Z39.48 Standard

Produced and manufactured in the United States of America by
OSL PUBLICATIONS
*The publishing minitstry of The Order of Saint Luke*
P O Box 5506
Maryville Tennessee 37802

The Order of Saint Luke is a religious order dedicated to sacramental and liturgical scholarship, education and practice. The purpose of the publishing ministry is to put into the hands of students and practitioners resources which have theological, historical, ecumenical and practical integrity.

# CONTENTS

## The Sunday Service

# PREFACE

John Wesley's *Sunday Service of the Methodists in North America* is, in a sense, the last will and testament of the octogenarian patriarch of Methodism to his American followers. At the same time, the book is the foundation stone for subsequent Methodist worship in this country. Until the 1970s, material from the *Sunday Service* was American Methodism's chief link to the worship of the ancient Church, the funnel through which the whole history of Christian worship poured into local churches. Thus it is a pivotal document linking American Methodist worship to that of the Church Universal by way of the Anglican tradition.

In the years since the Second Vatican Council, broader contacts with the worship life of other Christians have reached American Methodism. Documents from the early Church, unknown to Wesley and his contemporaries, have reshaped the worship of the churches of the West. Hand in hand have come new developments in biblical and historical scholarship and in liturgical theology. In The United Methodist Church, the impact of such broader contacts with universal Christianity, in both its ancient and modern forms, is apparent in the 1989 edition of the *United Methodist Hymnal*. This volume reveals a breadth of scope impossible in Wesley's time, but one which he, almost certainly, would have welcomed warmly.

In the midst of the new reformation in word and sacrament of our times, it is vital in order to deepen and sustain such reforming that the people called Methodists keep contact with their own historical roots. And it is clear that any understanding of what is distinctive in Methodist worship must begin with Wesley's legacy. The *Sunday Service* is the heart of his bequest and manifests his intentions most explicitly. Unfortunately, of the two thousand copies of the *Sunday Service* printed in 1784 for shipment to America, only approximately thirty-nine survive, and these are seen by few. This facsimile edition

i

is intended to resolve that difficulty by making it possible for many to have access to an exact reproduction of one of the rare originals. This reproduction should be an important asset in commemorating American Methodism's independent existence.

In this edition, a 1784 copy of the *Sunday Service* has been reproduced in full with the exceptions of the epistles and gospels (which are notated and to be read in the King James Version,) and the Psalter (which is likewise notated.) Wesley's hymns have been reset. An introduction has been added to provide general information about the book. The notes highlight other specific matters, such as the significant changes that Wesley made from the BCP, and indicate many of his precedents. The prayer book used for comparison has been an edition published in Oxford in 1784. It was "Printed by W. Jackson and A. Hamilton, Printers to the University" and contains all the services Wesley used.

Thanks are due to Dr. Kenneth E. Rowe of Drew University Library for making available the copies used for reproduction from Drew's magnificent collection of Methodistica and for his continuing gracious help during my research. The courtesies of other librarians at Seabury-Western Theological Seminary, Pierpont Morgan Library, Union Theological Seminary, United Methodist Publishing House, Candler School of Theology, Boston University School of Theology, General Theological Seminary, and Perkins School of Theology have enabled me to inspect personally sixteen of the surviving copies of the 1784 edition. Professors A. Raymond George, Frank Baker, and Richard P. Heitzenrater have read the manuscript and contributed from their great stores of learning. E. Farley Sharp has devoted much patient expertise in producing clear reproductions from often unclear originals. I appreciate greatly the efforts of Timothy J. Crouch, O.S.L., Director of Publications for The Order of Saint Luke, who added the collects, lesson notations and "A Collection of Psalms and Hymns," for making this edition possible.

James F. White
University of Notre Dame
November 1, 1995

ii

# INTRODUCTION

John Wesley's *Sunday Service* is, as its name indicates, a service book rather than a prayer book. It is intended to be used on the Lord's Day for public worship; only the litany is directed to be read on other days ("on Wednesdays and Fridays") and prayer is to be "extempore on all other days." Except for Christmas Day, Good Friday, and Ascension Day, no provision is made for weekday use, and the occasional services occur only as needed. The only exception to the sole use on Sunday in public worship is the provision of an abbreviated Psalter. This is structured for morning and evening prayer readings over a thirty-day period, but with no further instructions about its intended use. We may presume that the Psalter was to be used in private with daily extempore prayer. But the Psalter has been censored of Psalms and verses "highly improper for the mouths of a Christian Congregation," a phrase which suggests that it is intended for weekly corporate use rather than in daily private devotions.

Wesley's effort to provide worship forms for "those poor sheep in the wilderness" takes into account the radically different situation in the "States" where English civil and ecclesiastical authority had vanished "by a very uncommon train of providences." Wesley prunes away all the paraphernalia of an established national church. He resolves the uncertainty (in 1784) as to the leaders of civil government in America with ambiguous prayers for "the Supreme Rulers of these United States."

Wesley recognized that social conditions, too, were radically different. His book was intended for itinerant preachers in the process of gathering congregations rather than for established clergy in parish churches. Although Wesley's services follow formal structures from the *Book of Common Prayer* (BCP hereafter), his *Sunday Service* adds provision for the elder to "put up an Extempore Prayer" at the eucharist, and his letter suggests the same for weekday prayer. The absence of any choral bodies in American Methodism is acknowledged in changing all rubrics which read: "Then shall be said or sung" to abundant congregational song in the form of hymnody is presupposed by *A Collection of Psalms and Hymns for the Lord's Day* bound with the *Sunday Service*. Wesley's distaste for anthems as inappropriate for "joint worship" is evident in his act of discarding the rubric: "In Quires and Places where they sing, here followeth the Anthem" from both morning and evening prayer. Hymnody, which Wesley believed accessible to all, has replaced service music and anthems.

Wesley's sending of the hymnal along with the prayer book is significant. Congregational song was to be an integral part of Methodist worship. But *A Collection of Psalms and Hymns for the Lord's Day* was not a success although it was reprinted in 1791. It was soon superseded by various editions of *A Pocket Hymn Book* which John Wesley himself had revised in 1787 from a 1781 version put together by a printer in York named Robert Spence. The *Pocket Hymn Book* was popular and remained in use in America until 1821.

Little is presupposed architecturally. Rubrics about the arrangement of liturgical space are usually eliminated except for a few, very few, essential references: "The Elder, kneeling down at the Table," or "The Minister coming to the Font." Many references, but not all, to kneeling are removed. The most surprising remnant of a settled society is the retention of the marriage banns which "must be published in the Congregation, three several Sundays, in the Time of Divine Service: although the term "Congregation" has supplanted "Church." Mention of the church building disappears from the burial of the dead although one rubric suggests procession, probably to the building, while another indicates a different location, "At the Grave." All references to clerical garb are carefully eliminated throughout the *Sunday Service*. In short, a minimum of musical talent and architectural resources are needed for the worship Wesley envisions for North America. Flexibility and adaptability are provided for instead.

Notwithstanding all of Wesley's political, ecclesiastical, and cultural adaptations, his service book is a deeply conservative work, the product of one deeply, though not uncritically, enamored of the BCP. Every page of the *Sunday Service* bears marks, not of a casual reviser, but of one who had read or heard the prayer book daily throughout eight decades, and who is determined to retain all that wore well and to discard only that which proved inadequate in his own experience. Wesley's Preface indicates his conviction that no ancient or modern liturgy "breathes more of a solid, scriptural, rational Piety than the Common Prayer of the Church of England," and such a feeling is certainly witnessed to by his editing the prayer book for "our Societies in America." Wesley treats the BCP is "our incomparable liturgy" as had Anglicans long before his birth. Thus, if one sets aside the necessary political, ecclesiastical, and cultural changes, it is basically a conservative revision (in some ways more so even than the proposed 1786-BCP of the Protestant Episcopal Church). Wesley's conservatism is most apparent in the treatment of the Lord's Supper. The 166 eucharistic hymns of the Wesleys allowed considerable enrichment of the doctrines expressed in the Anglican rite, but the rite itself was changed little theologically by Wesley. The *Sunday Service,* then, is basically the work of one who loved the BCP and was determined to preserve it for others by adapting it to their changed circumstances.

I

Certain mysteries remain with regard to the production of Wesley's book from its inception until it was accepted at the "Christmas Conference" of the new Methodist Episcopal Church in Baltimore on December 27, 1784. We may presume that Wesley made his changes in a copy of the prayer book and certainly one, such as the Oxford printing of 1784, that included the ordinal and Articles of Religion. Dr. Thomas Coke saw it through the printer, William Strahan's firm in London. The pages were shipped across the Atlantic unbound in order to avoid the extra duty on bound volumes and was bound in New York. In the process, some alterations were made but it is impossible to pronounce precisely by whom. Five years afterward, in a letter dated June 20, 1789, Wesley wrote that "Dr. Coke made two or three little alterations in the Prayer-Book without my knowledge. I took particular care throughout to alter nothing merely for altering's sake. In religion I am for as few innovations as possible. I love the old wine best. And if it were only on this account, I prefer 'which' before 'who art in heaven,'"[1] Since editions also were published in 1786 and 1788, also with Coke's assistance, it is difficult to be certain that it was Coke who was responsible for the changes in 1784, although it seems likely. Nor does Wesley recollect, apparently, that he had himself changed the Lord's Prayer at two minor points throughout the book: "which" to "who art" and "in earth" to "on earth".

A mystery in the 1784 printing involves the elimination and restoration of the manual acts in the prayer of consecration at the eucharist and the sign of the cross in the rite of infant baptism. On the basis of the conservatism expressed in Wesley's 1789 letter, it seems most likely that he preferred to retain the manual acts and the sign of the cross, that Coke deleted both, and that Wesley sent along corrected sheets (following his original intentions) with the insistence that they be substituted for the defective pages 135-36 and 141-44 when the books were bound in America.[2] Not all were inserted as intended. Both versions exist today, one with all the original and corrected pages (Pierpont Morgan Library) and another with both sets of pages 135-36 (Pittsburgh Theological Seminary). The manual acts appear in subsequent editions, but the signation disappears, and such has been the situation throughout Methodist history until the 1970s. Variety also exists in the presence or absence of both Wesley's letter to the Methodist clergy in "North America" of September 10, 1784, and his preface dated the day before.

Adoption by the 1784 Christmas Conference by no means insured widespread use of the *Sunday Service,* although copies were kept in

---

[1] *Letters,* edited by John Telford (London: Epworth Press, 1931), VIII, 144-45

[2] This theory has been confirmed by the research of J. Hamby Barton, "The Two Versions," *Methodist History,* 23 (April, 1985), 153-162

print for American use during Wesley's lifetime. Subsequent editions specifically intended for American use were published in 1786 bearing the subtitle: *In the United States of America* and, in 1790: *In the United States of America...The Fourth Edition.* Other editions appeared in 1788 and 1792, some copies of which were intended for American use. But after the death of Wesley and the 1792 General Conference, the 314- page *Sunday Service* virtually disappeared except for 37 pages of "Sacramental Services &c." and the "Articles of Religion." The services underwent many alterations over the years, were eventually renamed "The Ritual," and remained in the *Discipline* until 1968. Jesse Lee, one of the early Methodist clergy, explained the *Sunday Service's* disappearance in that many of his fellow ministers felt "they could pray better, and with more devotion while their eyes were shut, than they could with their eyes open. After a few years the prayer book was laid aside, and has never been used since in public worship."[3] Its popularity in England was more durable as evidenced by fifteen additional printings in the first half of the nineteenth century. But the services were retained in the *Discipline* - baptism of infants and adults, eucharist, weddings, funerals, and ordinations - and have been the permanent basis of those rites for American Methodists until today. American editions of the whole book appeared in 1867 and 1893. In understanding prayer book revision, Wesley was indulging in a popular eighteenth-century pastime. No previous English prayer book had lasted in legal use for more than half a century, but the 1662 BCP was already into the third decade of its second century. It is still in use in England today. Anglicans, dissenters, even Benjamin Franklin, were publishing proposals for revisions. In April, 1754 Wesley had read with considerable sympathy the Puritan proposals for revision made at the Savoy Conference in 1661 prior to publication of the 1662 BCP. Known as the "Exceptions of the Ministers,"[4] these consist of ninety-six items on which Puritans of Presbyterian persuasion had

---

[3] *A Short History of the Methodists* (Baltimore:Magill and Clime, 1810), p. 107.
[4] Cf. Edward Cardwell, *A History of Conferences*, (Oxford:University Press, 1849), pp. 303-35.

tried, mostly in vain, to shape the 1662 BCP. A still earlier Puritan agenda appears in the "Millenary Petition" of 1603. Both documents are reflected at many points in Wesley's service book.

Although the 1662 BCP basically held the line against both the Laudian "high church" party and the Puritans, efforts were not long in appearing for a more comprehensive prayer book. An abortive effort in 1668 led to a more vigorous but equally unsuccessful attempt in 1689 at what might be called a "liturgy of comprehension."[5] The same year saw the suspension of the non-juring bishops and clergy. Freed from the state church, these men increasingly turned to the review of ancient liturgies, recovering many items overlooked in the English liturgical tradition. Nor were the non-jurors the only connoisseurs of early liturgies. As the scientific study of liturgies began to develop late in the seventeenth century, ancient texts that were not available to the compilers of 1662 became known. Writers of a variety of theological complexions produced their own proposals, often reflecting more liberal attitudes to doctrinal statements in line with the age of reason.

William Whiston, a mathematician and Anglican clergyman, adapted the fourth-century *Apostolic Constitutions* in 1713 to produce *The Liturgy of the Church of England, Reduc'd Nearer to the Primitive Standards.* Wesley had read (with major reservations) the 1749 plea for reform of a fellow Anglican priest, John Jones, which was contained in his much-discussed *Free and Candid Disquisitions Relating to the Church of England and the Means of Advancing Religion Therein.* A private revision of the BCP with Unitarian leanings was published in 1774 by Theophilus Lindsey, an Anglican priest turned Presbyterian minister. Lindsey combined materials from Samuel Clarke, John Jones, and others with his own ideas to produce *The Book of Common Prayer Reformed According to the Plan of the Late Dr. Samuel Clarke.* Many other attempts at private revision were familiar to Wesley as well as recently prepared services in actual use in the Episcopal Church of Scotland. The efforts of all these disparate groups - Puritans, comprehensionists, non-jurors, scholars of ancient

[5] T. J. Fawcett, *The Liturgy of Comprehension,* 1689 (London: Alcuin Club, 1973)

liturgies, and theological liberals - were known and read by Wesley. Evidences of his familiarity with a variety of sources appear in his revision, indicating that it is a well-researched effort, not personal whim. Wesley apparently refers to the Puritan "Exceptions" of 1661 in a letter of 1775: "Those ministers who truly feared God near an hundred years ago had undoubtedly much the same objections to the Liturgy which some (who never read their Works) have now. And I myself so far allow the force of several of those objections that I should not dare to declare my assent and consent to that book in the terms prescribed."[6] The oath of "unfeigned assent and consent to all and everything contained and prescribed" in the 1662 book had led to the ejection from their churches of both of Wesley's grandfathers. Ordained as fellow of a college, Wesley had not been put to the same test. But the sufferings of his Puritan ancestors is vindicated in Wesley's service book.

Although the Puritan "Exceptions" underlie many of Wesley's revisions, *Service* reflects far more than just the Puritan strain, although that certainly is present. Had Wesley's book been available a century and a quarter earlier, it might well have been acceptable to many desiring a comprehensive national church.

In a paper prepared for the Conference in 1755,[7] Wesley cited some of his objections to the BCP, the "damnatory clauses" in the Athanasian Creed, laudatory references to Charles II, the answers of the sponsors in baptism, confirmation itself, the absolution in the visitation of the sick, the thanksgiving prayer in the burial of the dead, anything pertaining to differences between bishops and presbyters in the ordinal, and the mention of "whatsoever sins ye remit, they are remitted" in the ordination of priests. All these features vanish in his own revision done almost thirty years later.

It is obvious that Wesley also had a concern for brevity and shortened many items. A major problem was the Anglican practice of actually reading three services each Sunday morning: morning prayer, the litany, and the first portion of the holy communion or

---

[6] *Letters,* III, 152.

[7] Cf. "Ought We to Separate from the Church of England?" in Frank Baker's *John Wesley and the Church of England* (Nashville:Abingdon Press, 1970), p. 331.

7

ante-communion (known then as the "second service"). As Wesley indicated in his preface, "The service of the LORD'S DAY, the length of which has been often complained of, is considerably shortened." Wesley's proposal still seems lengthy to modern eyes: he shortened morning prayer, relegated the litany to Wednesdays and Fridays only, and advised "the elders to administer the supper of the Lord on every Lord's day." Abridgment occurs, but it is in order to accommodate that rarity in eighteenth-century Anglicanism, a weekly eucharist. Hence it seems more accurate to refer to Wesley's book as a "revision" rather than as an "abridgment." Priorities have been shifted from those manufactured by conventional Anglican practice of the time in order to achieve a weekly eucharist.

Despite his own disclaimer in the 1789 letter, Wesley's services, like those of most of his contemporary revisers, reflect 120 years of change in the English language itself. Not only is the Lord's Prayer updated, but elsewhere phrases such as "who be" are modernized to "who are" and "charity" frequently becomes "love." There is wholesale redistribution of punctuation marks throughout, especially commas and semicolons, so that readings are recast in more current cadences. Needless to say, all references to the British government or the Church of England disappear or are replaced by American equivalents. The *Sunday Service* is an up-date version of the familiar 1662 BCP even though it retains so much of the earlier volume. Wesley's conservatism is moderated by the need to be contemporary.


II


Wesley's service book is a prime source for liturgical theology, i.e., theology based on the liturgical witness to faith. The distinctive element of the whole Wesleyan movement are shown in the way Wesley orders worship. The *Sunday Service* thus provides important data for theological reflection today. The liturgical circle begins by observing that which is said and done in worship as a reflection of belief, then examines systematically such evidence of faith, and finally reforms worship itself so as to express that faith more adequately. We can only briefly sketch here the evidence to faith found in the *Sunday Service*, and shall not discuss its contribution to liturgical reform at all. (The "Articles of Religion," as revised by Wesley, are an entirely different kind of evidence of belief, one which we shall not consider here.) Wesley's liturgical documentation of faith stands as a challenge in our day, both to theological reflection and to the reform of worship.

The basic pattern, of course, remains that of Anglican practice and faith. Wesley, in his preface, testifies to belief that the prayer book was not exceeded in terms of "solid, scriptural, rational Piety" by any other liturgy whether ancient or modern. Yet his emendations of the BCP are systematic and consistent. The faith that Wesley witnesses to in these pages is obviously uncomfortable with some aspects of prevailing piety and thoroughly at home with others. Rather than analyze Anglican piety in general, we must be content to look more closely at these elements in which Wesley differed from the BCP and made his differences evident by revision. We shall try to deduce his liturgical theology on the basis of what he retains, revises, and omits.

First of all, Wesley's vision for the Christian life is firmly built upon the God-given means of grace, particularly sacrament, scripture, and prayer. (Fasting is mentioned once for "All Fridays in the year, except Christmas-day.") Wesley's pattern for the Christian life is based on a community gathering each Sunday for morning and evening prayer, and celebrating the Lord's Supper "on every Lord's day." At a time when most Anglican parishes were content with three per year, Wesley's advice and his own practice were indeed revolutionary. He himself was not content with only a weekly eucharist but communed, more often not, twice a week.[8]

Scripture there was in abundance in Wesley's services: a lesson from the Old Testament was provided for each Sunday both for morning and evening prayer in his table of proper lessons; abundant psalmody was arranged over a thirty-day period; and the liturgical epistles and gospels were retained as provided in the BCP. A note

[8] John Bowmer, *The Sacrament of the Lord's Supper in Early Methodism* (London:Dacre Press, 1951), p. 55.

9

suggests that a gospel chapter be read at morning prayer and an epistle chapter at evening prayer. By far the largest portions of the book are devoted to selections from Scripture.

Prayer, too, abounds, not only in the Lord's Day service but in the litany for use on Wednesdays and Fridays and the call for extempore prayer on all other days. The *Sunday Service* calls for a highly disciplined life, structured on the appointed means of grace and lived in Christian community.

The whole focus of the book is strongly christological. Gone is the entire sanctoral (saints' days) cycle. Wesley felt that "most of the holy-days (so called)" were "at present answering no valuable end." Even the abbreviation "St." disappears with few exceptions (pp.133-298). The focus instead, is on Sunday as the day of resurrection, or "Lord's Day," as the Puritans demanded and Wesley often calls it. Even some of the christological festivals such as Epiphany, Maundy Thursday, and All Saints' Day disappear together with the Epiphany, pre-lenten, and Lent seasons. The year focuses on the birth and resurrection cycles, with Sundays numbered after Christmas and Easter as well as after Trinity Sunday. The only exceptions to the exclusively Sunday scheme (all of them christological) are Christmas Day, Good Friday, and Ascension Day.

For the Lord's Day, the traditional Anglican lections and collects are retained with only minor adjustment to accommodate Wesley's method of numbering Sundays after Christmas until "The Sunday next before Easter." It is significant that the Sunday lectionaries for morning and evening prayer and the eucharist are left intact. Christ's work is presented in orderly and systematic recital as the basis for reading and preaching.

Wesley did, however, take to pruning the Psalter rather severely. Of the 150 psalms in BCP, he excises 34 (or more than fifth) entirely. Verses disappear from another 58, to make a shrinkage from 2,502 verses in the BCP to 1,625 in the *Sunday Service*. This means a move from about 42 verses per service in the BCP to just under 28. William N. Wade[9] has analyzed the deletions as falling into five general

---

[9] Cf. his important dissertation "A History of Public Worship in the Methodist Episcopal Church and Methodist Episcopal Church, South from 1784 to 1905" (University of Notre Dame, 1981), pp. 52-76.

categories: curses, wrath, killing, and war; descriptions of the wicked, lack of faith, or special personal circumstances; at odds with salvation by faith; concerns exclusively historical or geographical, especially pertaining to Jerusalem; and references to the use of instruments of dance in worship. Wesley defended his exclusions, stating that there were "many Psalms left out, and many parts of the others, as being highly improper for the mouths of a "Christian Congregation." He also occasionally made changes in the translation, using the King James Version for a verse when it made better sense.

Wesley is certainly not the first (nor the last) to be troubled by untoward portions of the Psalter.[10] His preference for literal interpretations makes allegory unpalatable, and so he prunes away what seems inappropriate for common worship. The high value Wesley placed on the "Select Psalms" should not be overlooked, for they are by far the largest single items in the *Sunday Service*. Wesley had recited the psalms daily throughout his life. They were a major ingredient in his personal formation and he intended to transmit such a tradition, reformed to make it even better.

Ever since 1603 the Puritans had urged that "canonical Scriptures only be read in the Church." Wesley consistently avoids readings from the Apocrypha with one exception: Tobit 4:8-9 is retained as an offertory sentence at the eucharist, although the previous verse is eliminated. No mention of the Apocrypha appears in the "Articles of Religion."

Wesley's perception of the nature of ministry is apparent throughout the book. He prefers the term "Minister" in morning and evening prayer, the litany, and the occasional services. Only in the eucharist and at a few points in the ordinal is "elder" specified. The "superintendant [sic] has a special ministry as indicated throughout the ordinal, and a "deacon" is designated to read the gospel at his own ordination. There are significant shifts away from signs of priestly power. The words "priest" or "curate" disappear completely as the Puritans had argued in 1661 they should. "Bishop" also has been eliminated completely. No references to clerical garb or ornaments appears.

---

[10] A topic on the agenda of the first synod of Roman Catholic bishops in 1967.

The term "absolution" has gone entirely. Wesley declared in *Popery Calmly Considered:* "For judicially to pardon sin and absolve the sinner, is a power God has reserved to himself." At morning and evening prayer, the collect from the 24th Sunday after Trinity is substituted for the absolution; at the eucharist the absolution is made into a prayer by changing the pronouns to "thy" and "thou," while the elder identifies with the people by use of "us" instead of "you."

More freedom is allowed the minister in some instances. The elder "if he see it expedient, may put up an Extempore Prayer" at the eucharist (although unmentioned elsewhere in the services). The Puritans had pled in vain for such freedom. Likewise a sermon is to be preached at the eucharist. Wesley eliminates any mention of using one of the printed homilies from the sixteenth century which BCP suggested. The rather tedious exhortations are scrapped at eucharist and baptism. Sixteenth-century didacticism has been put to rest in these instances, although similar elements, such as the Decalogue at the eucharist or charges at matrimony and at ordination, are retained.

A significant shift occurs in the way the process of becoming a Christian is signified. The concept of baptismal regeneration, although biblical (John 3:5; Titus 3:5) is problematic for Wesley because of his emphasis on the personal experience of conversion. Wesley keeps the declaration in the "Articles of Religion" that baptism "is a sign of regeneration, or the new birth." But he does make more moderate the references to baptismal regeneration in the rites of infant and adult baptism themselves without eliminating such references altogether. The opening statement in the infant baptism rite and the prayer after the gospel both refer to regeneration as taking place in baptism. But after the act of baptism, in the statement after the signation "that *this Child* is regenerate and grafted," the words "regenerate and" disappear. In the prayer after the Lord's Prayer, "that it hath pleased thee to regenerate *this Infant* with thy Holy Spirit." Presumption that regeneration is inevitable seems offensive to Wesley, and so any suggestion of such is abolished. Similar disappearances occur in the adult rite: "that *these Persons* are regenerate" loses "regenerate and," and the "now" in "that being

12

now born again'' vanishes. In short, Wesley does not eliminate the concept of baptismal regeneration but seems to remove any presumption on it. The 1786 edition makes further changes. Criticism of the doctrine of baptismal regeneration was common in liberal theological circles in Wesley's time and broke out in the Gorham dispute within the Church of England in the 1840s.

Wesley's omissions are often important statements themselves. The most baffling of these is his omission of a rite of confirmation. Eighty years later, the Methodist Episcopal Church found it advisable to add a service for the ''Reception of Members'' and a century after that this was renamed ''Confirmation.'' The value of a separate rite of confirmation has long been problematic. The Puritans had asked in the millenary Petition of 1603 that ''confirmation, as superfluous, may be taken away.'' Apparently it had been little administered prior to the reign of James 1. Wesley indicated his opposition to confirmation in his paper for the Conference of 1755. Perhaps Wesley anticipated the misgivings of modern theologians about confirmation and felt it better to exclude it rather than to perpetuate the mistakes of the middle ages and reformation. At any rate, exclude it he did but with no mention of his reasons for so doing.

Wesley's other omissions are significant but less puzzling. The legal documents often bound in eighteenth-century BCPs, the table of contents, the various Acts of Uniformity, ''the Preface,'' ''Concerning the Service of the Church,'' ''Of Ceremonies,'' and the instructions on reading the Psalter and scripture lessons, Wesley recognized as irrelevant to the American situation. The daily calendar and tables and rules for the feasts and fasts were not necessary for a Sunday service book. Like many of his contemporaries, Wesley was happy to be rid of the so-called Athanasian Creed.

Private baptism he omitted without indicating just why. Probably Wesley had a sound liturgical instinct that a baptism ought to be public. The catechism requisite to confirmation also disappears. Similarly absent is visitation of the sick although Wesley keeps communion of the sick. ''The Thanksgiving of Women after Childbirth'' disappears. Wesley eliminated Ash Wednesday so there is no need for ''A Commination, or Denouncing of God's Anger and

13

Judgments against Sinners,'' appointed for that day. ''Forms of Prayer to be used at Sea'' also is removed.

It should be no surprise that the vehemently nationalistic state services, included by royal edict in eighteenth-century BCPs, should be removed. Gunpowder treason, the execution of one English monarch, the restoration of another, and the accession of a third (and the hated George III at that) would hardly appeal to Americans. Episcopalians toyed with services for July 4 and Thanksgiving Day, but only the latter made it into their 1789 book. Wesley did not try to anticipate American festivals but otherwise accommodated to a new country and its distinctive situation.

# NOTES

*[Ed. Note: We regret the uneven quality that appears from time to time in the original material. These sections were photographed from a 1784 edition and appear here as they do there.]*

*Letter of Sept. 10, 1784.* This letter appears in most, but not all, surviving copies, sometimes bound before the title page, sometimes after it.

*Title page.* The name of the publisher, William Strahan, is omitted.

*Preface,* p. [1]. This preface is found in most copies but not all. At least four different printings survive.

*Proper LESSONS to be read at Morning and Evening Prayer,* pp. [3-5]. Wesley omits the usual BCP instructions ("the Order how"), the daily calendar, and the tables and rules of the feasts. Only three pages of twenty dealing with propers survive. The thirty-three BCP holy days have largely disappeared, and the three that remain (other than Sundays) are referred to on page [5] simply as "particular Days" instead of "Holy Days." "Ash Wednesday" has been removed from Wesley's "Proper PSALMS on Certain Days." The Puritan "Exceptions" of 1661 urged "that the religious observation of saints-days appointed to be kept as holy-days, and the vigils thereof, without any foundation (as we conceive) in Scripture, may be omitted." The lessons for the three "particular Days" Wesley retains remain unchanged. Of the "Proper PSALMS on certain Days" six psalms disappear, all ones Wesley removes from his Psalter: 21, 54, 88, 108, 110, and 132.

The most radical change in the table of lessons is in the calendar. The seasons of Epiphany, Pre-Lent, and Lent have been expunged in favor of numbering fifteen Sundays after Christmas plus the "Sunday before Easter" (Lent 6). The missing Sunday is Lent 5. This leaves Wesley short one Sunday although this would be a problem only in years when Easter came later than mid-April. The idea may have come from Whiston's revision of 1713 which numbered Sundays after Epiphany right through Lent. Other than this one drastic change before Easter, Wesley's calendar is that of the BCP for Sundays. Wesley's suppression of Lent is in line with a long succession of Puritan objections, including the "Exceptions" against "the observation of Lent as a religious fast, the example of Christ's fasting forty days and nights being no more imitable, nor intended for the imitation of a Christian, than any other of his miraculous works were."

Wesley has updated "Mattins" and "Evensong" in the table to "Morning" and "Evening." Wesley's only changes in the lessons themselves are to leave out Exodus 3 and 5 (previously Lent 5). Genesis 7 and 18 are substitutes for Genesis 9:1-20 and Genesis 12 on the eleventh Sunday and Genesis 24 and 37 take the place of Genesis 27 and Genesis 34 on the thirteenth Sunday. Genesis 44 is added to Genesis 45 on the fifteenth Sunday. The only clear pattern in Wesley's alterations of lessons seems to be the desire to find more edifying passages in place of some less so, such as Genesis 34.

Wesley added a rubric about the New Testament lesson. This rubric is a great simplification of the daily lectionary in "The Calendar with the Table of Lessons" which Wesley omits. Apparently, for Wesley's Sunday services the lessons to be read "in regular Rotation" indicates readings chosen at the minister's discretion and no indication is given as to the meaning of "where it is otherwise provided." An abridgment of a similar rubric in BCP on fasting is shortened by including Lent, the Ember Days, and the three Rogation Days but retaining the Friday fast.

*The ORDER for MORNING PRAYER, Every Lord's Day*, pp. [7]-14. A major change occurs in the function, as reflected by the subtitle, indicating a weekly service rather than "Daily throughout the Year."

Because he proposes an exclusively Sunday service to be used in conjunction with the Lord's Supper, Wesley makes some abridgments. In 1603 the Puritans had urged that "the longsomeness of service [be] abridged," and Wesley noted such a concern in his Preface. Accordingly, the *Venite*, second Lord's Prayer, suffrages, anthem, and two prayers are eliminated and the psalm readings shortened. But the excisions have been done with a careful hand. The opening rubrics about the place where prayers were to be said and about the ornaments of the church and ministers' garb have disappeared, probably because Wesley found them meaningless in America and unenforced in England. The penitential opening of 1552 survives with a minimum of change: six of the opening sentences vanish for no apparent reason, and a sentence that had listed the acts of worship -confession, thanksgiving, praise, hearing the Word, and petition - disappears from the call to confession. No changes appear in the general confession itself, but the rather didactic BCP absolution has been replaced by the collect for Trinity 24 (unchanged) and the rubrics are made simpler and less priestly. (Theophilus Lindsey's revision of 1774 had constituted the Collect for Purity, instead.)

Deviations are more pronounced in the original 1549 opening which begins with the Lord's Prayer, The *Venite* and accompanying rubric are omitted altogether even though Psalm 95 appears uncut in Wesley's Psalter. Probably the last four wrathful verses suggested removal of the whole *Venite* to Wesley; these verses were replaced in the 1789 American BCP. The rubric about the *Gloria Patri* omits the words "throughout the year," and apparently it is to be said in unison. The Old Testament lesson is to be found in the weekly "Table of proper Lessons: rather than in the daily Calendar. No rubric about announcing and terminating lessons remains. Likewise gone is the option of the lengthy canticle from the Apocrypha *Benedicite, omnia opera Domini.* The briefer *Te Deum Laudamus* remains. After the second lesson the option of the *Benedictus* (Luke 1:68-79) is lacking, while the *Jubilate Deo* (Psalm 100) survives. The Puritans in 1661 had objected to the *Benedicite* as "apocryphal" and the attempted liturgy of comprehension of 1689 suggested elimination of all New Testament canticles but the *Magnificat,* doubtless in response to Puritan pressures.

The prayers lack the second Lord's Prayer, the suffrages, and the prayers for the royal family and for clergy and people. The second and third collects are no longer daily obligations but remain unchanged to be said weekly, "all devoutly kneeling." No mention is made of an anthem in line with Wesley's conviction that "they cannot properly be called joint worship," nor do the rubrics indicate that any canticles or creed be sung. A shortened version of the prayer for the King's Majesty has become "for the Supreme Rulers." It now intercedes for "the Supreme Rulers of these United States" (the first use of that term in a prayer book). This prayer and that of St. Chrysostom (now untitled) are kept for weekly use. The apostolic benediction, II Corinthians 13:14, remains, except that here and elsewhere Wesley replaces "you" with "us" following more closely the Greek text. The final rubric omits the words "throughout the Year."

*The ORDER for EVENING PRAYER, Every Lord's Day.* , pp. 14-19. Changes parallel to those in morning prayer occur here. After the first lesson, the *Magnificat* (Luke 1:46-55) is not printed but only the second choice, *Cantate Domino,* Psalm 98. Verses 6 and 7 are omitted as in Wesley's Psalter in accord with his omission of reference to musical instruments. After the New Testament lesson, the *Nunc dimittis* (Luke 2:29-32) likewise disappears, leaving *Deus misereatur* Psalm 67) as the only choice. No reference is made to kneeling for the collects at evening prayer. The Lord's Prayer remains unrevised from BCP here but nowhere else, a slip-up corrected in 1786. The Athanasian Creed, appointed to be read on thirteen occasions in the year by BCP, disappears entirely. The Puritans had objected to it in 1661 and Wesley in 1755 explained his concurrence in its doctrines but not in *"the damnatory clauses."*

*The LITANY,* pp. 20-26. The opening rubric omits mention of use on "Sundays, Wednesdays, and Fridays, and at other times," most likely in line with Wesley's concern about the length of the Sunday service. His letter of Sept. 10, 1784 reaffirms the use of the litany on "Wednesdays and Fridays," and it remains in the ordination rites. The petition for King George is redirected to "the supreme Rulers of these United States." Three subsequent petitions -for the King, royal family, and Lords and nobility - disappear. Another petition, that for "Bishops, Priests, and Deacons," becomes "all the Ministers of thy Gospel." Otherwise the litany remains virtually untouched with the exception of minor emendations.

18

*A PRAYER and THANKSGIVING, to be used every Lord's Day,* pp, 26-27. Of the collection of nineteen prayers appointed in BCP, for use at the litany or at morning and evening prayer, Wesley retains for weekly use but two: the "prayer for all conditions of men" and the General Thanksgiving.

*THE COLLECTS, EPISTLES, AND GOSPELS, to be used throughout the Year,* pp.. 27-124 (not printed in this edition). Wesley's chief changes are those in the calendar. Gone are all the saints' days plus weekday, holy days such as Circumcision, Epiphany, Presentation, Ash Wednesday, Annunciation, All Saints' Day, and the lesser days of Holy Week, Easter Week, and Whitsun Week. Christmas Day, Good Friday, and Ascension Day alone remain. Sundays are numbered "after Christmas" until "The Sunday next before Easter." The BCP collect, epistle, and gospel for the first Sunday after the Epiphany provides Wesley's second Sunday after Christmas propers. (The 1661 BCP had no Christmas 2 propers, simply reusing Circumcision, which Wesley expunges.) The language of the collects and lections is occasionally updated as in the changes from "charity" to "love" on the Tenth Sunday after Christmas. Anthems are retained to "be said" at morning prayer before the psalms on Easter Day. The twenty-five Sundays after Trinity remain unchanged except for minor updating of words, punctuation, and capitalization. Except for the removal of holy days and saints days, this is the most conservative part of Wesley's service book and shows his love of the Cranmerian collects and traditional lections. (His treatment of the Psalter is radical by comparison).

Wesley omits the general rubric about the use of collects for the vigil or eve of Sunday and holy days. Rubrics about daily use of the Advent 1, Nativity, Circumcision, and Ash Wednesday collects are also missing. A final rubric about the Twenty-fifth Sunday after Trinity is omitted. This BCP rubric provides for the use of propers of unused Sundays after Epiphany if the Trinity Sunday ran long in any year. The twenty-fifth Sunday's "stir up" collect and lections were to be always "used upon the Sunday next before Advent," another rubric that Wesley omits. At morning and evening prayer he had provided for twenty-six Sundays after Trinity. His scheme for the eucharist could run short some years in the post-Christmas and post-Trinity seasons.

*The Order for the Administration of the LORD'S SUPPER,* pp. 125-139. See Appendix I for pages 135-36 of what we presume was the first printing. The pages that follow contain the manual acts as probably inserted at Wesley's command. The Puritans generally favored the manual acts, as did most Anglicans, and it is difficult to see why they were retracted in the first printing.

Wesley's treatment of the Lord's Supper is deeply conservative; no really essential matters are altered in it. The long didactic exhortations disappear plus an optional post-communion prayer. Minor adaptions to the American situation occur, but basically the 1662 rite remains intact. Wesley's excision of all the collect printed at the end "to be said after the Offertory, when there is no Communion" is another indication of his determination to have a weekly eucharist.

The title has been shortened, removing the words "or Holy Communion" but "the Communion" appears in the running heads of each page and "Holy Communion" is in several rubrics. The first three general rubrics are omitted, the first, about giving prior notice of intention to commune, was probably deemed difficult in an itinerant situation and the others, dealing with the "open and notorious evil liver" and unreconciled persons, could be dealt with in Methodist class meetings. The remaining rubric deals with the location of the Lord's table, but Wesley is less specific and eliminates the obsolete reference to north- side celebration, an archaism of the 1662 BCP. Individual rubrics are shortened and simplified throughout and the location of action is not indicated.

No changes appear in the Decalogue. One of the two collects for the King disappears while the other is altered to "the Supreme Rulers of these United States." The Nicene Creed is omitted, presumably because the Apostles' Creed would have been said already at morning prayer. A long rubric about announcements is omitted and a sermon is mandatory (as the "Exceptions" urged it should be), and no mention is made of the printed homilies. Of the twenty offertory sentences BCP provides, Tobit 4:7 is omitted but the 4:8-9 verses remain, the only use of the Apocrypha in the *Sunday Service* and a passage specifically decried by the "Exceptions." A different translation of I Timothy 6:6-7 is provided. The rubric about the placing of the bread and wine upon the table, a rubric which suggests the possibility of no communion, disappears entirely.

The prayer for the "Whole State of Christ's Church" is altered only to revise allusions to King George, "the whole Council," and to "Bishops and Curates." Wesley apparently felt that the people called Methodists had no need for the long extortions BCP provides to give "warning" of an upcoming celebration of the holy communion (especially when he desired weekly celebrations), about lax attendance at the sacrament, or for serious preparation for reception of the sacrament. The invitation is unchanged but in the general confession, the sentence: "The burden of them is intolerable" disappears, as it had in Lindsey's 1774 version. The absolution is turned into a prayer by adding "O" and by changing the pronouns (again, following Lindsey on the pronouns). Wesley, who removed many inferences to posture, adds an "all standing" rubric for the Comfortable Words and "The People also kneeling" for the Prayer of Humble Access.

The Eucharistic Prayer remains untouched save for the removal of a redundant "one" in the post-Sanctus. All references to weekday celebration are excluded from the proper preface as in the "Exceptions." In the preface for Christmas Day: "Of the substance of the Virgin Mary his mother" is removed. The rubric which comes just before the Prayer of Consecration fails to mention "ordering" the bread and wine. Wesley places the fraction three words later than in BCP.

In the communion rubric, "all meekly kneeling," so offensive to the Puritans, disappears. A theological shift occurs in the rubric about reconsecration: Wesley opts for repeating the entire so-called "Prayer of Consecration" rather than just the words of institution (BCP) indicating a move away from the medieval and Lutheran attitude that the verbs effected consecration rather than the whole act of thanksgiving. (This had the support of the 1689 attempt at revision, Whiston, and the Scottish communion rite of 1764.)

21

The original conclusion of the eucharistic prayer in 1549 is retained as a post-communion prayer and the other option, the 1549 post-communion prayer, is dropped (as in Lindsey). The *Gloria in excelsis* is said, not sung. A new rubric now provides for "Extempore Prayer" if the elder "see it expedient." The concluding blessing adds the word "May" to make it more of a prayer than a benediction. Wesley omits nine rubrics dealing with occasions without communion, the necessary number of communicants, provision, quality, and consumption of the bread and wine, mandatory communion thrice yearly, and money offerings. Gone also is the 1662 statement about kneeling which declares "no adoration is intended" to the bread and wine. Wesley expected the singing of eucharistic hymns, but they are not mentioned in the service itself.

The MINISTRATION of BAPTISM of INFANTS, pp. 139-43. See pages 141-44 of what is presumably the first printing. In the pages that follow, the signation occurs.

Major changes, theological and practical, occur in the rite of infant baptism. The doctrine of baptismal regeneration is not expressed after baptism but is clearly stated before the act of baptism. Godparents are eliminated although at the baptism there is reference to "Friends of the Child." But neither is mention made of the parents, as the Puritans advocated. The rite is shortened losing the more didactic elements.

Wesley omits rubrics about baptism being in public on Sundays or holy days as well as the word "PUBLICK" in the title (although it appears in the running heads on each page) and the subtitle "To be used in the CHURCH" disappears. He provides no service for "The MINISTRATION of PRIVATE BAPTISM of Children IN HOUSES," probably not wanting to encourage such practice and in accord with the "Exceptions" mention of "no need" for such a rite. No provisions are made for emergency baptism. Gone also are rubrics about godparents and about giving the curate forewarning and being ready after the last lesson at morning or evening prayer. The opening question: "Hath this child been already baptized, or no? is eliminated, probably as unnecessary.

Wesley's rite follows unchanged the BCP address which mentions regeneration by water and Spirit. The "flood" prayer is almost untouched as is the succeeding collect with its mention of "spiritual regeneration" despite Puritan exception to these very words. After the gospel (Mark 10:13-26) the exhortation is removed but the following prayer with petition "that *he* may be born again" remains. The address to the godparents disappears together with the renunciation and questions as to faith (the Apostles' Creed) and ethics, responded to formerly by godparents. Almost thirty years before Wesley had objected to "the answers...made by the sponsors." The prayers after the creed remain unchanged. The prayer over the font (lost in American Methodism from 1916 to 1976) remains scarcely changed from BCP. Wesley's conservatism is evident in retaining the rubric about baptism by dipping, a practice going into disuse in Anglicanism at that time. But he does give sprinkling as an alternative and subsequent editions recover the BCP option of pouring. The signation occurs unchanged except for a superfluous "do." As early as the Millenary Petition of 1603, the Puritans had objected to "the cross in baptism" as well as "interrogatories ministered to infants" (which Wesley does omit). The sign of the cross along with kneeling at the eucharist were the object of the most vehement of Puritan objections, and it is remarkable that Wesley (apparently) retains the signation in 1784 but was persuaded to relinquish it in subsequent editions.

The theology of regeneration is moderated in the post-baptismal prayers. In the first, a blunt statement of regeneration - "regenerate and" - disappears as do the words, to which the Puritans had objected, "regenerate...with thy Holy Spirit" from the final prayer. Gone also is the final exhortation to the godparents about teaching the catechism and bringing the child to confirmation. Two final rubrics vanish, those concerning children dying baptized and explaining the sign of the cross by referring to the canons of 1604.

*The MINISTRATION of BAPTISM to such as are of RIPER YEARS,* pp. 143-49. This rite, new to the Church of England in 1662, reflects the growing awareness of mission. In Wesley's version, changes take place similar to those at infant baptism, except that there is no mention whatsoever of signation. The phrase "And able to answer for themselves" disappears from the title. Wesley omits the opening rubrics about notification of the bishop, time of celebration, and previous baptism, all of little necessity in America. No changes appear in the opening address, flood prayer, second prayer, and gospel (John 3:1-8). The exhortation is removed but the following prayer that "*they* may be born again" remains. Minor changes happen in the address to the candidates. Wesley retains the renunciation and credal and ethical questions with "flesh" changed to "body" in the Creed. The prayers which follow remain intact.

Only the references to godparents is changed in the baptismal rubrics. Dipping or pouring is specified, with no mention of sprinkling. All reference to the sign of the cross is missing. In the three final prayers, "regenerate and" disappear from the first and the "now" is removed in the third from the phrase "being now born again." Two final exhortations to godparents and the new Christians are removed, as well as two final rubrics on confirmation and the baptism of children older than infants.

Two significant omissions occur in subsequent pages: Wesley's removal of "A CATECHISM" and that for which it prepared, "THE ORDER OF CONFIRMATION." Wesley's actions are clear in removing confirmation, but his reasons are not.

The Form of Solemnizaton of MATRIMONY, pp. 149-55, Wesley changes little in the marriage service although he does omit the giving away of the bride, the exchange of rings, the psalms, and the final exhortation. A surprising survival is the reading of the banns, although no mention is made of reading them at the offertory at the second service (BCP). Legal details about the banns disappear from the rubrics, as well as all indications that the first part of the service takes place "In the body of the Church." The address to the congregation survives intact contrary to Wesley's usual removal of didactic exhortations. The long rubric about impediments is excised.

The betrothal vows are unchanged and lead immediately into the nuptial vows with no giving-away ceremony, a change for which

Wesley seems to have no precedent. In the second vows "troth" becomes "Faith" and a "be" is added: "Take thee M. to be my..." The long rubric and words which accompany the giving of the ring are absent, as is any reference to this action in the prayer and pronouncement that follow. The Millenary Petition of 1603 had asked that "the ring in marriage...may be corrected" and the "Exceptions" reiterate this. The service is shortened after the blessing by elimination of Psalm 128 or 67, although Wesley printed both in his Psalter. No rubric mentions he move to the Lord's table which the 1662 BCP had retained despite Puritan protests. Only minor changes appear in the Kyrie, Lord's Prayer, suffrages, and the three final prayers. Wesley makes no mention of a sermon and removes the long exhortation on "the duties of Man and Wife." The final rubric, advising the couple to receive communion then or shortly thereafter, is removed as the Puritans had suggested it be.

Wesley omits altogether *"THE ORDER FOR The VISITATION of the SICK."* He had objected in 1755 to "the *absolution* in the Office for visiting the sick," an objection his Puritan forebears had raised in 1661.

*The COMMUNION of the SICK*, pp. 155-56. Wesley's rite is identical with the brief Anglican rite, lacking only the long introductory rubric which gives details about circumstances of celebration and where to begin, and the three last of the final rubrics on the impossibility of communing in certain situations, the use of the visitation rite, and "in time of Plague, Sweat," or such contagion.

*The Order for the BURIAL of the DEAD*, pp. 156-61. Beyond omission of the committal and thanksgiving, only minor changes take place in this rite. Most references to location in church or churchyard are missing. The opening rubric, disallowing the use of the service for the unbaptized, excommunicate, or suicides, is deleted. The choice of psalms is reduced to one (Psalm 90) although BCP gives Psalm 39 first and Wesley does include it in his Psalter. The psalm and epistle (I Corinthians 15:20-58) have minor changes in translation.

The rubric after the epistle presumes that the previous part of the service was held inside the church but abbreviates the BCP wording. The committal is omitted together with the rubric about casting earth. The prayer which follows the Lord's Prayer is removed, Wesley having complained in 1755 about "the thanksgiving in the *Burial Office.*" Absent from the final collect are two clauses: "who also hath taught us, by his holy Apostle Saint Paul, not to be sorry, as men without hope, for them that sleep in him" and "as our hope is this our *brother* doth." Wesley may have hesitated to sound so certain about the eternal destination of the departed as these deleted items suggest. The Puritan "Exceptions" had feared that these items might "harden the wicked" and urged their revision.

Two other pastoral offices are omitted: "THE Thanksgiving of Women After Child-Birth" and A COMMINATION OR Denouncing of God's Anger and Judgments against Sinners." The first is a short office consisting of Psalm 116 or 127 (to which Wesley took no exception), Kyrie, Lord's Prayer, suffrages, and prayer of thanksgiving. Wesley's reasons for omitting this service are unclear. Since he had eliminated Ash Wednesday and Lent, no purpose would be served by the commination rite. Wesley must have found repugnant its curses from Deuteronomy 27, for he had removed similar images of divine wrath from the Psalter. (Lindsey also deleted both services).

*SELECT PSALMS*, pp, 162-279 (not printed in this edition). The largest single item in Wesley's service book is his abridgment and editing of "The PSALTER OR PSALMS OF DAVID, pointed as they are to be sung, or said in Churches." Wesley retains the daily distribution of psalms for both morning and evening prayer over a thirty-day period. He omits the Latin titles for each psalm.

Wesley eliminates entirely thirty-four psalms (14, 21, 52, 53, 54, 58, 60, 64, 72, 74, 78, 79, 80, 81, 82, 83, 87, 88, 94, 101, 105, 106, 108, 109, 110, 120, 122, 129, 132, 134, 136, 137, 140, and 149). In addition, portions of 58 others disappear. (The chief reasons for these deletions have been listed in the Introduction). The net result is to reduce the number of verses read by about one third. Wesley numbers the verses retained consecutively with no indication of verses omitted.

Occasionally the BCP translation is replaced by that of the King James Version.

For reasons unknown, Wesley omitted completely "Forms of PRAYER to be used at SEA." The prayers for "His Majesty's Navy" obviously would have had little appeal to Americans.

*The Form and Manner of making of DEACONS*, pp. 280-85. In many printings of the BCP, the ordinal is omitted. Where present, an entire page is often given to the title and "THE PREFACE." The BCP preface defends a three-fold ministry, gives minimum ages for each ministry, and speaks to the examination of candidates and times of ordination. Wesley makes a distinction from the rest of the service book simply by two large rules at the top of the page, similar to those which mark off the "Articles of Religion" on page 306. His title for the whole ordinal dispenses with the words "and Consecrating" and "According to the Order of the Church of England." Here and elsewhere, Wesley changes "Bishops" to "Superintendants" *[sic]* and "Priests" to "Elders." Throughout he removes all references to the English Church and its structures and changes "Ordering" to "Ordaining." All references to clerical garb are struck from the rubrics. All three services begin with morning prayer, and the ordinations are all in the context of holy communion. For the ordination of deacons and elders, the sermon follows morning prayer; for superintendents, it comes after the gospel. The rite of deacons begins (after abbreviated rubrics) without the presentation. Wesley omits reprinting the litany (pp. 20-26). BCP reprints it, adding a new petition for deacons (or priests) but omitting the final prayer and benediction. Wesley retains these last two items but excludes them (by rubric) in the elders' rite. The order of the whole service is similar to that of the usual Sunday practice of the Church of England - morning prayer, litany, and eucharist - and leads naturally to the collect for the eucharist.

The collect and epistle (I Timothy 3:8-13) are unchanged although the alternative (Acts 6:2-7) is missing. The "Oath of the Kings Sovereignty" necessarily disappears. Changes in the examination reflect the American situation with the total effect that the deacon's duties and whereabouts are less circumscribed. The duty of expounding the scripture is added without qualification and "read homilies" deleted.

The laying on of hands does not specify that the candidates kneel and, in the formula,"committed unto thee" is omitted. The words at the deliverance of the Bible (not the "New Testament" as in BCP) do not limit preaching by the phrase "if thou be thereto licensed by the bishop himself." The gospel is the same (Luke 12:35-38) and Wesley indicates that communion is to follow immediately, not just "the same day." Wesley removes the final rubric about waiting a year before being ordained priest.

*The Form and Manner of ordaining of ELDERS*, pp, 285-96. Many of the same changes are made for elders as for deacons although the rubrics are less altered. The chief theological change is in the omission from the formula at the laying on of hands: "Whose sins thou dost forgive, they are forgiven; and whose sins thou dost retain, they are retained" (John 20:23). Wesley had objected to this in 1755 on theological grounds. The restriction to ministering to the congregation "where thou shall be lawfully appointed thereunto" could hardly survive the scrutiny of one who deemed the whole world his parish. The shorter alternative gospel Matthew 9:36-38, and the Nicene Creed are also omitted.

The second rubric is shortened as is the presentation. A new rubric is added:"their Names being read aloud." The inquiry about impediments speaks of "this day to ordain Elders," instead of "to receive this day into the holy Office of Priesthood." A clause is dropped from the epistle (Ephesians 4:7-13). Curiously the long exhortation remains, only one word being changed. The third question of the examination is shortened drastically and, in the fourth, "Cures" becomes "district." Only one translation, that of Bishop Cosin, is given here and at the superintendents' rite for the *Veni, Creator Spiritus*. The communion rubric and final rubric are simplified.

*The Form of Ordaining of a SUPERINTENDANT,* pp. 296-305. Much in the title changes but little in the service itself. Wesley's title

28

is an abridgment of "The FORM of Ordaining or Consecrating OF AN ARCHBISHOP OR BISHOP: Which is always to be performed upon some SUNDAY or HOLY- DAY." Throughout, Wesley drops the term "consecrate" and "Superintendant" [sic] takes the place of "Archbishop." Elders assist the presiding superintendent in the laying on of hands and perform some of the other functions BCP ascribes to bishops.

The short Timothy 3:1-7 epistle option is dropped. John 20:19-23 disappears as a gospel option, doubtless because of its mention of forgiveness and retention of sins. Wesley, for once, allows two BCP options instead of one: John 21:15-17 or Matthew 28:18-20. The Nicene Creed is absent.

At the presentation the candidate is described as "godly" but Wesley leaves out "and well-learned." The King's Mandate, the Oath of the King's Supremacy, and the Oath of due obedience to the Archbishop have no place in Wesley's version. No petition is added to the litany similar to that which BCP provides for this occasion. At the beginning of the examination "and the ancient Canons" is omitted and "diocese" becomes "district" in the sixth question. In the charge at the giving of the Bible, "and be diligent in doing them" is removed. Wesley makes it clear that "other Persons present" are also to communicate.

Four nationalistic services which in BCP follow are discarded: gunpowder treason, death of Charles I, restoration of Charles II, and accession of George III.

*ARTICLES OF RELIGION*, pp. 306-41. Wesley's revision of the Articles is one of the most sweeping in the whole book. Thirty-nine articles are reduced to twenty-four (another is added in subsequent editions) and many of the survivors are abridged or altered. As might be expected, the Royal Declaration of George III is omitted. The ratification by convocation in 1571 and the table of the articles also disappear. Wesley's intent in revision seems to be to insist only on central Christian doctrines and to avoid unnecessary controversy.

Those articles which are excised entirely are: Of the going down of Christ into Hell; Of the three Creeds; Of Works before Justification;

29

Of Christ alone Without Sin; Of Predestination and Election; Of obtaining eternal Salvation only by the Name of Christ: Of the authority of the Church; Of the Authority of General Councils; Of Ministering in the Congregation; Of the Unworthiness of the Ministers, which hinder not the effect of the Sacraments; Of the Wicked, which eat not the Body of Christ in the use of the Lord's Supper; of excommunicate Persons, how they are to be avoided; Of the Homilies; of Consecration of Bishops and Ministers; and Of the Civil Magistrates.

We shall follow Wesley's numbering of the remaining articles in examining major changes. In V, all mention of the Apocryphal books disappears. Number VII is much abridged, losing all mention of God's wrath and damnation but vehemently affirming human inclination to evil by adding "and that continually." IX avoids any mention of the homilies. A change is made in the name and contents of XII from "Of Sin after Baptism: to "Of Sin after Justification" with the term "justification" substituted throughout for "baptism." A condemnation of the Church of Rome in XIII is dropped. In XVI Wesley omits "sure witnesses and effectual" after "but rather they be certain" and before "Signs of Grace."

Major surgery occurs in XVII. "Christened" becomes "baptized." After "new birth" Wesley omits mention of any benefits received from Baptism other than regeneration. The list in BCP includes: "whereby as by an instrument, they that receive Baptism rightly are grafted into the Church; the promises of forgiveness of sin, and of our adoption to be the sons of God by the Holy Ghost, are visibly signed and sealed; Faith is confirmed, and Grace increased by virtue of prayer unto God." In the final sentence, Wesley drops "in any wise" and "as most agreeable with the institution of Christ." The total effect is to weaken somewhat the teaching of the efficacy of baptism. By contract, Article XVIII, on the Lord's Supper, remains intact.

In XIII "rites and ceremonies: is substituted for "Traditions" and the mention of the magistrate and "man's authority" vanishes. Reference to "certain *Anabaptists*" disappears in XXIII.

"A TABLE of KINDRED and AFFINITY," usually bound in BCPs, is omitted in Wesley's *Sunday Service*. Whereas the usual BCP close is "The End," Wesley, for once, prefers a Latin word as his final word: "FINIS."

## SELECT BIBLIOGRAPHY

Baker, Frank, *From Wesley to Asbury*. Durham: Duke University Press, 1976.

_____, *John Wesley and the Church of England*. Nashville:Abingdon Press, 1970.

_____, *A Union Catalogue of the Publications of John and Charles Wesley*. Durham: Divinity School, Duke University, 1966.

English, John C. "The Sacrament of Baptism according to the Sunday Service of 1784," *Methodist History*, V (January, 1967), 10-16.

Cardwell, Edward. *A History of Conferences and Other Proceedings Connected with the Revision of the Book of Common Prayer from the Year 1558 to the Year 1690*. Third Edition. Oxford: University Press, 1849.

Cuming, G. J. *A History of Anglican Liturgy*. Second Edition. London: Macmillan, 1982.

Fawcett, Timothy J. *The Liturgy of Comprehension of 1689*. London:Alcuin Club, 1973.

Gee, Henry and Hardy, William John. *Documents illustrative of English Church History*. Macmillan & Co., 1910.

George A. Raymond, "The 'Sunday Service,'"*Proceedings of the Wesley Historical Society*, XL (February, 1976), 137-44.

_____, "The Sunday Service of the Methodists," *Communion Sanctorum: Melanges offerts a Jean Jacques von Allmen*. Geneva: Labor et Fides, 1982, pp. 194-203.

_____, "The Sunday Service 1784," *Friends of Wesley Chapel Annual Lecture No. 2*, n.p., 1983.

Grisbrooke, W. Jardine. *Anglican Liturgies of the Seventeenth and Eighteenth Centuries*. London: SPCK, 1958.

Hall, Peter. *Documents Illustrative of the Liturgy of the Church of England*. Vol. VII *Dunkirk Prayer-book*. Bath: Binns and Goodwin, 1848.

_____, *Reliquae Liturgicae, Documents Connected With the Liturgy of the Church of England*. Vol. IV *The Savoy Liturgy*. Bath: Binns and Goodwin, 1847.

Harmon, Nolan B. "John Wesley's 'Sunday Service' and its American Revisions," *Proceedings of the Wesley Historical Society*, XXXIX (June, 1974), 137-44

_____, *Rites and Rituals of Episcopal Methodism,* Nashville: Publishing House of the M.E. Church, South, 1926.

Hatchett, Marion J. *The Making of the First American Prayerbook.* Ann Arbor: University Microfilms, 1973; New York: Seabury Press, 1982.

Hunter, Frederick. "Sources of Wesley's Revision of the Prayer Book in 1784-8." *Proceedings of the Wesley Historical Society,* XXIII (1941-42), 137- 44.

Peaston, A. Elliott. *The Prayer Book Tradition in the Free Churches.* London: James Clarke & Co., 1964.

Spellman, Norman. "The Formation of the Methodist Episcopal Church," *The History of American Methodism.* Nashville: Abingdon Press, 1964, I, 185-232.

Swift, Wesley F. "John Wesley's Lectionary," *London Quarterly & Holborn Review* CLXXXIII (October, 1958), 298-304.

_____, Methodism and the Book of Common Prayer," *Proceedings of the Wesley Historical Society,* XXVII (1949-50), 33-41.

_____, "'The Sunday Service of the Methodists,'" *Proceedings of the Wesley Historical Society,* XXIX (March, 1953), 12-20.

_____, "The "Sunday Service of the Methodists,'" *Proceedings of the Wesley Historical Society,* XXXII (March, 1960), 97-101.

Thompson, Bard. *Liturgies of the Western Church.* Cleveland: Collins, 1961.

Wesley, John. *The Letters.* Edited by John Telford. London: Epworth Press, 1931. 8 volumes.

To Dr. COKE, Mr. ASBURY, and our Brethren in *NORTH-AMERICA*.

1. **B**Y a very uncommon train of providences, many of the provinces of *North-America* are totally disjoined from their mother-country, and erected into Independent States. The Englifh government has no authority over them either civil or ecclefiaftical, any more than over the States of *Holland*. A civil authority is exercifed over them, partly by the Congrefs, partly by the provincial Affemblies. But no one either exercifes or claims any ecclefiaftical authority at all. In this peculiar fituation fome thoufands of the inhabitants of thefe States defire my advice; and in compliance with their defire, I have drawn up a little fketch.

2. Lord KING's account of the primitive church convinced me many years ago, that Bifhops and Prefbyters are the fame order, and confequently have the fame right to ordain. For many years I have been importuned from time to time, to exercife this right, by ordaining part of our travelling preachers. But I have ftill refufed, not only for peace' fake: but becaufe I was determined, as little as poffible to violate the eftablifhed order of the national church to which I belonged.

**a**  3. But

3. But the cafe is widely different between England and North-America. Here there are Bifhops who have a legal jurifdiction. In America there are none, neither any parifh minifters. So that for fome hundred miles together there is none either to baptize or to adminifter the Lord's fupper. Here therefore my fcruples are at an end : and I conceive myfelf at full liberty, as I violate no order and invade no man's right, by appointing and fending labourers into the harveft.

4. I have accordingly appointed Dr. COKE and Mr. FRANCIS ASBURY, to be joint *Superintendents* over our brethren in North-America : As alfo RICHARD WHATCOAT and THOMAS VASEY, to act as *Elders* among them, by baptizing and adminiftering the Lord's fupper. And I have prepared a liturgy little differing from that of the church of England (I think, the beft conftituted national church in the world) which I advife all the travelling-preachers to ufe, on the Lord's day, in all their congregations, reading the litany only on Wednefdays and Fridays, and praying extempore on all other days. I alfo advife the elders to adminifter the fupper of the Lord on every Lord's day.

5. If any one will point out a more rational and fcriptural way, of feeding and guiding thofe poor fheep in the wildernefs, I will gladly

gladly embrace it. At prefent I cannot fee any better method than that I have taken.

6. It has indeed been propofed, to defire the Englifh Bifhops, to ordain part of our preachers for *America*. But to this I object, 1. I defired the Bifhop of *London*, to ordain only one; but could not prevail: 2. If they confented, we know the flownefs of their proceedings; but the matter admits of no delay. 3. If they would ordain them *now*, they would likewife expect to govern them. And how grievoufly would this intangle us? 4. As our *American* brethren are now totally difentangled both from the State, and from the Englifh Hierarchy, we dare not intangle them again, either with the one or the other. They are now at full liberty, fimply to follow the fcriptures and the primitive church. And we judge it beft that they fhould ftand faft in that liberty, wherewith GOD has fo ftrangely made them free.

JOHN WESLEY.

# THE

# SUNDAY SERVICE

OF THE

# METHODISTS

IN

# NORTH AMERICA.

With other Occasional Services.

LONDON:

Printed in the Year MDCCLXXXIV.

I BELIEVE there is no LITURGY in the World, either in ancient or modern language, which breathes more of a folid, fcriptural, rational Piety, than the COMMON PRAYER of the CHURCH of ENGLAND. And though the main of it was compiled confiderably more than two hundred years ago, yet is the language of it, not only pure, but ftrong and elegant in the higheft degree.

Little alteration is made in the following edition of it, (which I recommend to our SOCIETIES in AMERICA) except in the following inftances :

1. Moft of the holy-days (fo called) are omitted, as at prefent anfwering no valuable end.

2. The fervice of the LORD's DAY, the length of which has been often complained of, is confiderably fhortened.

3. Some fentences in the offices of Baptifm, and for the Burial of the Dead, are omitted.—And,

4. Many Pfalms left out, and many parts of the others, as being highly improper for the mouths of a Chriftian Con-gregation.

*John Wefley.*

*Briftol, Septemben 9,*
*1784.*

| Proper _LESSONS_ to be read at _Morning_ and _Evening_ Prayer, on the _SUNDAYS_ throughout the _Year._ | | |
|---|---|---|
| _Sundays of Advent._ | _Morning._ | _Evening._ |
| The firſt. | Iſaiah —— 1 | Iſaiah —— 2 |
| 2 —— | —— 5 | —— 24 |
| 3 —— | —— 25 | —— 26 |
| 4 —— | —— 30 | —— 32 |
| _Sundays after Chriſtmas._ | | |
| The firſt | —— 37 | —— 38 |
| 2 —— | —— 41 | —— 43 |
| 3 —— | —— 44 | —— 46 |
| 4 —— | —— 51 | —— 53 |
| 5 —— | —— 55 | —— 56 |
| 6 —— | —— 57 | —— 58 |
| 7 —— | —— 59 | —— 64 |
| 8 —— | —— 65 | —— 66 |
| 9 —— | Geneſis 1 | Geneſis 2 |
| 10 —— | —— 3 | —— 6 |
| 11 —— | —— 7 | —— 18 |
| 12 —— | 19 to ver. 30 | —— 22 |
| 13 —— | —— 24 | —— 37 |
| 14 —— | —— 39 | —— 42 |
| 15 —— | —— 43 | —— 44 & 45 |
| _Sunday before Eaſter._ | | |
| 1 Leſſon. | Exodus 9 | Exodus 10 |
| 2 Leſſon. | Matth. 26 | Heb. 5 to v. 11 |
| _Eaſter day._ | | |
| 1 Leſſon. | Exodus 12 | Exodus 14 |
| 2 Leſſon. | Rom. 6 | Acts 2 v. 22 |
| _Sundays after Eaſter._ | | |
| The firſt. | Numb. 16 | Numb. 22 |
| 2 —— | —— 23 & 24 | —— 25 |
| 3 —— | Deuter. 4 | —— 5 |
| 4 —— | —— 6 | —— 7 |
| 5 —— | —— 8 | —— 9 |
| _Sunday after Aſcenſion day._ | —— 12 | Deuter. 13 |
| _Whitſunday._ | | |
| 1 Leſſon. | —— 16 to ver. 18 | Iſaiah 11 |
| 2 Leſſon. | Acts 10 ver. 34 | Acts 19 to ver. 21 |

## Proper Leſſons for Sundays.

| Trinity-Sunday | Morning. | | Evening. | |
|---|---|---|---|---|
| 1 Leſſon. | Geneſis | 1 | Geneſis | 18 |
| 2 Leſſon. | Matth. | 3 | 1 John | 5 |
| Sundays after Trinity Sunday. | | | | |
| The firſt. | Joſhua | 10 | Joſhua | 23 |
| 2 ——— | Judges | 4 | Judges | 5 |
| 3 ——— | 1 Sam. | 2 | 1 Sam. | 3 |
| 4 ——— | ——— | 12 | ——— | 13 |
| 5 ——— | ——— | 15 | ——— | 17 |
| 6 ——— | 2 Sam. | 12 | 2 Sam. | 19 |
| 7 ——— | ——— | 21 | ——— | 24 |
| 8 ——— | 1 Kings | 13 | 1 Kings | 17 |
| 9 ——— | ——— | 18 | ——— | 19 |
| 10 ——— | ——— | 21 | ——— | 22 |
| 11 ——— | 2 Kings | 5 | 2 Kings | 9 |
| 12 ——— | ——— | 10 | ——— | 18 |
| 13 ——— | ——— | 19 | ——— | 23 |
| 14 ——— | Jerem. | 5 | Jerem. | 22 |
| 15 ——— | ——— | 35 | ——— | 36 |
| 16 ——— | Ezekiel | 2 | Ezekiel | 13 |
| 17 ——— | ——— | 14 | ——— | 18 |
| 18 ——— | ——— | 20 | ——— | 24 |
| 19 ——— | Daniel | 3 | Daniel | 6 |
| 20 ——— | Joel | 2 | Micah | 6 |
| 21 ——— | Habak. | 2 | Prov. | 1 |
| 22 ——— | Prov. | 2 | ——— | 3 |
| 23 ——— | ——— | 11 | ——— | 12 |
| 24 ——— | ——— | 13 | ——— | 14 |
| 25 ——— | ——— | 15 | ——— | 16 |
| 26 ——— | ——— | 17 | ——— | 19 |

☞ Let the Second Leſſon in the Morning be a Chapter out of the Four Goſpels, and the Acts of the Apoſtles; and the Second Leſſon in the Evening be a Chapter out of the Epiſtles, in regular Rotation; excepting where it is otherwiſe provided.

## Proper *LESSONS for particular Days.*

| Nativity of Christ. | Morning. | Evening. |
|---|---|---|
| 1 Leſſon. | Iſaiah 9 to v. 8 | Iſaiah 7 v. 10. to (v. 17 |
| 2 Leſſon. | Luke 2 to v. 15 | Tit. 3 v. 4 to v. 9 |
| *Good Friday.* | | |
| 1 Leſſon. | Gen. 22 to v. 20 | Iſaiah 53 |
| 2 Leſſon. | John 18 | 1 Peter 2 |
| *Aſcenſion-day.* | | |
| 1 Leſſon. | Deuter. 10 | 2 Kings 2 |
| 2 Leſſon. | Luke 24 v. 44. | Eph. 4 to v. 17. |

## Proper *PSALMS on certain Days.*

| | Morning. | Evening. |
|---|---|---|
| *Chriſtmas-day.* | Pſalm 19 <br> ——— 45 <br> ——— 85 | Pſalm 89 <br> ——— <br> ——— |
| *Good Friday.* | Pſalm 22 <br> ——— 40 | Pſalm 69 <br> ——— |
| *Eaſter-day.* | Pſalm 2 <br> ——— 57 <br> ——— 111 | Pſalm 113 <br> ——— 114 <br> ——— 118 |
| *Aſcenſion-day.* | Pſalm 8 <br> ——— 15 | Pſalm 24 <br> ——— 47 |
| *Whit-ſunday.* | Pſalm 48 <br> ——— 68 | Pſalm 104 <br> ——— 145 |

## *Days of Faſting or Abſtinence.*

All the Fridays in the Year, except *Chriſtmas-day.*

A 3

# The ORDER for
# MORNING PRAYER,
### Every Lord's Day.

*At the Beginning of Morning Prayer, the Minister shall read with a loud Voice some one or more of these Sentences of the Scriptures that follow : And then he shall say that which is written after the said Sentences.*

WHEN the wicked man turneth away from his wickedness that he hath committed, and doeth that which is lawful and right, he shall save his soul alive. *Ezek.* xviii. 27.

The sacrifices of God are a broken spirit : a broken and a contrite heart, O God, thou wilt not despise. *Psal.* li. 17.

To the Lord our God belong mercies and forgivenesses, though we have rebelled against him : neither have we obeyed the voice of the Lord our God, to walk in his laws which he set before us. *Dan.* ix. 9, 10.

I will arise, and go to my father, and will say unto him, Father, I have sinned against Heaven and before thee, and am no more worthy to be called thy son. *Luke*, xv. 18, 19.

Enter not into judgment with thy servant, O Lord ; for in thy sight shall no man living be justified. *Psal.* cxliii. 2.

DEarly beloved brethren, the Scripture moveth us, in sundry places, to acknowledge and confess our manifold sins and wickedness, and that we should not dissemble-or cloke them before the face of Almighty God, our heavenly Father ; but

confess

confefs them with an humble, lowly, penitent, and obedient heart; to the end that we may obtain forgivenefs of the fame, by his infinite goodnefs and mercy.    Wherefore I pray and befeech you, as many as are here prefent, to accompany me with a pure heart and humble voice, unto the throne of the heavenly grace, faying after me.

*A general Confeffion, to be faid by the whole Congregation, after the Minifter, all kneeling.*

ALmighty and moft merciful Father, We have erred and ftrayed from thy ways like loft fheep.    We have followed too much the devices and defires of our own hearts.    We have offended againft thy holy laws.    We have left undone thofe things which we ought to have done;    And we have done thofe things which we ought not to have done;    And there is no health in us.    But thou, O Lord, have mercy upon us, miferable offenders.    Spare thou them, O God, which confefs their faults.    Reftore thou them that are penitent;    According to thy promifes declared unto mankind in Chrift Jefus our Lord.    And grant, O moft merciful Father, for his fake, That we may hereafter live a godly, righteous, and fober life;    To the glory of thy holy Name.    Amen.

*Then the Minifter fhall fay,*

O Lord, we befeech thee, abfolve thy people from their offences; that, through thy bountiful goodnefs, we may be delivered from the bands of thofe fins, which by our frailty we have committed.    Grant this, O heavenly Father, for Jefus Chrift's fake, our bleffed Lord and Saviour.

*The People fhall anfwer here, and at the End of all other Prayers.* Amen.

Then

*Then the Minister shall say the Lord's Prayer; the
People also repeating it with him, both here, and
wheresoever else it is used in Divine Service.*

OUR Father who art in Heaven, Hallowed
be thy Name; Thy kingdom come; Thy
Will be done on Earth, As it is in Heaven: Give
us this day our daily bread; And forgive us our
trespasses, As we forgive them that trespass against
us; And lead us not into temptation; But deliver
us from evil: For thine is the Kingdom, and the
Power, and the Glory, For ever and ever. Amen.

*Then likewise he shall say,*

O Lord, open thou our lips.
*Answ.* And our mouth shall shew forth thy praise.
*Minist.* O God, make speed to save us;
*Answ.* O Lord, make haste to help us.

*Here all standing up, the Minister shall say,*

Glory be to the Father, and to the Son, and
to the Holy Ghost;
*Answ.* As it was in the beginning, is now, and
ever shall be, world without end. Amen.
*Minist.* Praise ye the Lord.
*Answ.* The Lord's Name be praised.

*Then shall follow the Psalms, in order as they are ap-
pointed. And at the End of every Psalm, shall be
repeated,*

Glory be to the Father, and to the Son, and
to the Holy Ghost;
As it was in the beginning, is now, and ever
shall be, world without end. Amen.

*Then shall be read distinctly, the First Lesson taken out
of the Old Testament, as is appointed in the Table*

A 5 *of*

*of proper Leſſons : He that readeth, ſo ſtanding,
and turning himſelf as he may be beſt heard of all.
And after that, ſhall be ſaid the following Hymn :*

WE praiſe thee, O God : we acknowledge thee to be the Lord.

All the earth doth worſhip thee, the Father everlaſting.

To thee all Angels cry aloud : the Heavens, and all the powers therein.

To thee Cherubin and Seraphin continually do cry,

Holy, holy, holy, Lord God of Sabaoth ;

Heaven and Earth are full of the Majeſty of thy Glory.

The glorious company of the Apoſtles praiſe thee.

The goodly fellowſhip of the Prophets praiſe thee.

The noble army of Martyrs praiſe thee.

The Holy Church throughout all the world doth acknowledge thee ;

The Father of an infinite Majeſty ;

Thine honourable, true, and only Son ;

Alſo the Holy Ghoſt, the Comforter.

Thou art the King of glory, O Chriſt ;

Thou art the everlaſting Son of the Father.

When thou tookeſt upon thee to deliver man, thou didſt not abhor the Virgin's womb.

When thou hadſt overcome the ſharpneſs of death, thou didſt open the kingdom of Heaven to all believers.

Thou ſitteſt at the right hand of God, in the glory of the Father.

We believe that thou ſhalt come to be our Judge.

We

We therefore pray thee, help thy fervants, whom thou haft redeemed with thy precious blood.

Make them to be numbered with thy Saints in glory everlafting.

O Lord, fave thy people, and blefs thine heritage.

Govern them, and lift them up for ever.

Day by day we magnify thee ;

And we worfhip thy name ever, world without end.

Vouchfafe, O Lord, to keep us this day without fin.

O Lord, have mercy upon us : have mercy upon us.

O Lord, let thy mercy lighten upon us, as our truft is in thee.

O Lord, in thee have I trufted : let me never be confounded.

*Then fhall be read in like manner the Second Leffon, taken out of the New Teftament : and after that, the following Pfalm :*

O Be joyful in the Lord, all ye lands : ferve the Lord with gladnefs, and come before his prefence with a fong.

Be ye fure that the Lord he is God ; it is he that hath made us, and not we ourfelves : we are his people, and the fheep of his pafture.

O go your way into his gates with thankfgiving, and into his courts with praife : be thankful unto him, and fpeak good of his Name.

For the Lord is gracious, his mercy is everlafting : and his truth endureth from generation to generation.

Glory be to the Father, and to the Son, and to the Holy Ghoft ;

As it was in the beginning, is now, and ever fhall be, world without end. Amen.

*Then*

*Then shall be said the Apostles' Creed by the Minister and the People, standing.*

I Believe in God the Father Almighty, Maker of Heaven and Earth :

And in Jesus Christ his only Son our Lord ; Who was conceived by the Holy Ghost ; Born of the Virgin Mary ; Suffered under Pontius Pilate ; Was crucified, dead, and buried, He descended into hell : The third day he rose again from the dead : He ascended into Heaven, And sitteth on the right hand of God, the Father Almighty ; From thence he shall come to judge the quick and the dead.

I believe in the Holy Ghost ; The Holy Catholick Church ; The Communion of Saints ; The Forgiveness of Sins ; The Resurrection of the Body, And the Life everlasting.    Amen.

*And after that, the Minister shall pronounce with a loud Voice,*

The Lord be with you ;
*Answ.* And with thy spirit.

*Minister.*    Let us pray.
Lord, have mercy upon us.
*Answ.* Christ have mercy upon us.
*Minist.* Lord, have mercy upon us.

*Then shall follow three Collects ; the first of the Day, which shall be the same that is appointed at the Communion ; the second for Peace ; the third for Grace to live well ; all devoutly kneeling.*

*The second Collect, for Peace.*

O God, who art the author of peace, and lover of concord, in knowledge of whom standeth our eternal life, whose service is perfect freedom ; Defend us thy humble servants in all assaults of

6                                                    our

our enemies ; that we, furely trufting in thy defence, may not fear the power of any adverfaries, through the might of Jefus Chrift our Lord. *Amen.*

### The Third Colle&t, for Grace.

O Lord our heavenly Father, Almighty and everlafting God, who haft fafely brought us to the beginning of this day ; Defend us in the fame with thy mighty power ; and grant that this day we fall into no fin ; neither run into any kind of danger : but that all our doings may be ordered by thy governance, to do always that is righteous in thy fight, through Jefus Chrift our Lord. *Amen.*

### Then thefe Prayers following are to be read.

### A Prayer for the Supreme Rulers.

O Lord our heavenly Father, high and mighty, King of kings, Lord of lords, the only Ruler of princes, who doft from thy throne behold all the dwellers upon earth ; Moft heartily we befeech thee, with thy favour to behold the Supreme Rulers of thefe United States, and fo replenifh them with the grace of thy Holy Spirit, that they may alway incline to thy will, and walk in thy way; through Jefus Chrift our Lord. *Amen.*

ALmighty God, who haft given us grace at this time with one accord, to make our common fupplications uhto thee, and doft promife that when two or three are gathered together in thy Name, thou wilt grant their requefts ; Fulfil now, O Lord, the defires and petitions of thy fervants, as may be moft expedient for them : granting us in this world knowledge of thy truth, and in the world to come life everlafting. *Amen.*

*2. Cor.*

*2 Cor.* xiii 14.

THE grace of our Lord Jeſus Chriſt, and the love of God, and the fellowſhip of the Holy Ghoſt, be with you all evermore. *Amen.*

*Here endeth the Order of Morning Prayer.*

---

### The ORDER for
# EVENING PRAYER,
### Every Lord's Day.

*At the Beginning of Evening Prayer, the Miniſter ſhall read with a loud Voice ſome one or more of theſe Sentences of the Scriptures that follow : And then he ſhall ſay that which is written after the ſaid Sentences.*

WHEN the wicked man turneth away from his wickedneſs that he hath committed, and doeth that which is lawful and right, he ſhall ſave his ſoul alive. *Ezek.* xviii. 27.

The ſacrifices of God are a broken ſpirit : a broken and a contrite heart, O God, thou wilt not deſpiſe. *Pſal.* li. 17.

To the Lord our God belong mercies and for-giveneſſes, though we have rebelled againſt him : neither have we obeyed the voice of the Lord our God, to walk in his laws which he ſet before us. *Dan.* ix. 9, 10.

I will ariſe, and go to my father, and will ſay unto him, Father, I have ſinned againſt heaven and before thee, and am no more worthy to be called thy ſon. *Luke,* xv. 18, 19.

Enter not into judgment with thy ſervant, O Lord ; for in thy ſight ſhall no man living be juſtified. *Pſal.* cxliii. 2.

DEarly beloved brethren, the Scripture moveth us, in ſundry places, to acknowledge and confeſs our manifold ſins and wickedneſs ; and that

we

we fhould not diffemble nor cloke them before the face of Almighty God, our heavenly Father ; but confefs them with an humble, lowly, penitent, and obedient heart ; to the end that we may obtain forgivenefs of the fame by his infinite goodnefs and mercy. Wherefore I pray and befeech you, as many as are here prefent, to accompany me with a pure heart and humble voice, unto the throne of the heavenly grace, faying after me.

*A general Confeffion to be faid of the whole Congregation, after the Minifter ; all kneeling.*

ALmighty and moft merciful Father, We have erred and ftrayed from thy ways like loft fheep. We have followed too much the devices and defires of our own hearts. We have offended againft thy holy laws. We have left undone thofe things which we ought to have done ; And we have done thofe things which we ought not to have done ; And there is no health in us. But thou, O Lord, have mercy upon us, miferable offenders. Spare thou them, O God, which confefs their faults. Reftore thou them that are penitent ; According to thy promifes declared unto mankind in Chrift Jefus our Lord. And grant, O moft merciful Father, for his fake ; That we may hereafter live a godly, righteous, and fober life ; To the glory of thy holy Name. Amen.

*Then the Minifter fhall fay,*

O Lord, we befeech thee, abfolve thy people from their offences ; that, through thy bountiful goodnefs, we may be delivered from the bands of thofe fins, which by our frailty we have committed. Grant this, O heavenly Father, for Jefus Chrift s fake, our bleffed Lord and Saviour. *Amen.*

*Then*

*Then the Minister shall say the Lord's Prayer ; the People also repeating it with him.*

OUR Father which art in heaven, Hallowed be thy Name ; Thy kingdom come ; Thy will be done in earth, as it is in heaven : Give us this day our daily bread ; And forgive us our trespasses, as we forgive them that trespass against us : And lead us not into temptation ; But deliver us from evil : For thine is the Kingdom, and the Power, and the Glory, For ever and ever. Amen.

*Then likewise he shall say,*

O Lord, open thou our lips,

*Answ.* And our mouth shall shew forth thy praise.

*Minister.* O God make speed to save us.

*Answ.* O Lord make haste to help us.

*Here all standing up the Minister shall say,*

Glory be to the Father, and to the Son : and to the Holy Ghost ;

*Answ.* As it was in the beginning, is now, and ever shall be : world without end. Amen.

*Minister.* Praise ye the Lord.

*Answ.* The Lord's Name be praised.

*Then shall be said the Psalms in order as they are appointed. Then a Lesson of the Old Testament, as is appointed : And after that the following Psalm :*

O Sing unto the Lord a new song : for he hath done marvellous things.

With his own right hand, and with his holy arm ; hath he gotten himself the victory.

The Lord declared his salvation : his righteousness hath he openly shewed in the sight of the heathen.

He

He hath remembered his mercy and truth towards the houſe of Iſrael ; and all the ends of the world have ſeen the ſalvation of our God.

Shew yourſelves joyful unto the Lord, all ye lands : ſing, rejoice, and give thanks.

Let the ſea make a noiſe, and all that therein is; the round world and they that dwell therein.

Let the floods clap their hands, and let the hills be joyful together before the Lord : for he cometh to judge the earth.

With righteouſneſs ſhall he judge the world; and the people with equity.

Glory be to the Father, &c.

As it was in the beginning, &c.

*Then a Leſſon of the New Teſtament, as it is appointed: And after that the following Pſalm :*

GOD be merciful unto us, and bleſs us ; and ſhew us the light of his countenance, and be merciful unto us.

That thy way may be known upon earth ; thy ſaving health among all nations.

Let the people praiſe thee, O God : yea, let all the people praiſe thee.

O let the nations rejoice and be glad ; for thou ſhalt judge the folk righteouſly, and govern the nations upon earth.

Let the people praiſe thee, O God : yea, let all the people praiſe thee.

Then ſhall the earth bring forth her increaſe ; and God, even our own God, ſhall give us his bleſſing.

God ſhall bleſs us : and all the ends of the world ſhall fear him.

Glory be to the Father, &c.

As it was in the beginning, &c.

*Then*

*Then shall be said the Apostles Creed by the Minister
and the People ; standing.*

I Believe in God the Father Almighty, Maker of
Heaven and Earth :

And in Jesus Christ his only Son our Lord ; Who
was conceived by the Holy Ghost; Born of the Virgin Mary ; Suffered under Pontius Pilate; Was crucified, dead, and buried, He descended into hell :
The third day he rose again from the dead ;
He ascended into heaven, and sitteth on the right
hand of God the Father Almighty ; From thence
he shall come to judge the quick and the dead.

I believe in the Holy Ghost ; the Holy Catholic
Church , the Communion of Saints; The for-
giveness of sins ; The resurrection of the body ;
And the life everlasting.   Amen.

*Then shall the Minister pronounce with a loud Voice,*
The Lord be with you.
*Answ.* And with thy spirit.
*Minist.* Let us pray.
Lord, have mercy upon us.
*Answ. Christ, have mercy upon us.*
*Minist.* Lord, have mercy upon us.

*Then shall follow three Collects ; the first of the Day ;
the second for Peace, the third for aid against all
Perils.*

### The second Collect at Evening-Prayer.

O God, from whom all holy desires, all good
counsels, and all just works do proceed ; Give
unto thy servants that peace which the world cannot give ; that both our hearts may be set to obey
thy commandments, and also that by thee we
being defended from the fear of our enemies, may
pass our time in rest and quietness, through the
merits of Jesus Christ our Saviour.   *Amen.*

*The*

*The third Collect, for Aid against all Perils.*

Lighten our darkness, we befeech thee, O Lord; and by thy great mercy defend us from all perils and dangers of this night, for the love of thy only Son our Saviour Jefus Chrift. *Amen.*

*A Prayer for the Supreme Rulers.*

O Lord our heavenly Father, high and mighty, King of kings, Lord of lords, the only Ruler of princes, who doft from thy throne behold all the dwellers upon earth; Moft heartily we befeech thee, with thy favour to behold the Supreme Rulers of thefe United States; and fo replenifh them with the grace of thy Holy Spirit, that they may incline to thy will, and walk in thy way; through Jefus Chrift our Lord. *Amen.*

Almighty God, who haft given us grace, at this time, with one accord to make our common fupplications unto thee; and doft promife, that when two or three are gathered together in thy Name, thou wilt grant their requefts; Fulfil now, O Lord, the defires and petitions of thy Servants, as may be moft expedient for them; granting us in this world knowledge of thy truth, and in the world to come life everlafting. *Amen.*

2 Cor. xiii. 14.

THE grace of our Lord Jefus Chrift, and the love of God, and the fellowfhip of the Holy Ghoft, be with you all evermore. *Amen.*

*Here endeth the Order of Evening Prayer.*

*Here*

*Here followeth the LITANY, or General Supplication, to be said upon* Wednesdays *and* Fridays.

O God the Father of heaven ; have mercy upon us miserable sinners.

*O God the Father of heaven ; have mercy upon us miserable sinners.*

O God the Son, Redeemer of the world ; have mercy upon us miserable sinners.

*O God the Son, Redeemer of the world ; have mercy upon us miserable sinners.*

O God the Holy Ghost, proceeding from the Father and the Son ; have mercy upon us miserable sinners.

*O God the Holy Ghost, proceeding from the Father and the Son ; have mercy upon us miserable sinners.*

O holy, blessed, and glorious Trinity, three persons, and one God ; have mercy upon us miserable sinners.

*O holy, blessed, and glorious Trinity, three persons, and one God ; have mercy upon us miserable sinners.*

Remember not, Lord, our offences, nor the offences of our forefathers ; neither take thou vengeance of our sins : spare us, good Lord, spare thy people, whom thou hast redeemed with thy most precious blood, and be not angry with us for ever.

*Spare us, good Lord.*

From all evil and mischief ; from sin, from the crafts and assaults of the devil, from thy wrath, and from everlasting damnation,

*Good Lord, deliver us.*

From all blindness of heart ; from pride, vainglory, and hypocrisy ; from envy, hatred, and malice, and all uncharitableness,

*Good Lord, deliver us.*

From

From fornication, and all other deadly fin; and from all the deceits of the world, the flefh, and the devil,

*Good Lord, deliver us.*

From lightning and tempeft; from plague, peftilence, and famine; from battle and murder, and from fudden death,

*Good Lord, deliver us.*

From all fedition, privy confpiracy, and re-bellion; from all falfe doctrine, herefy and fchifm; from hardnefs of heart, and contempt of thy word and commandment,

*Good Lord, deliver us.*

By the myftery of thy holy Incarnation; by thy holy Nativity and Circumcifion; by thy Baptifm, Fafting, and Temptation,

*Good Lord, deliver us.*

By thine Agony and bloody Sweat; by thy Crofs and Paffion; by thy precious Death and Burial; by thy glorious Refurrection and Afcen-fion; and by the coming of the Holy Ghoft,

*Good Lord, deliver us.*

In all time of our tribulation; in all time of our wealth; in the hour of death, and in the day of judgment,

*Good Lord, deliver us.*

We finners do befeech thee to hear us, O Lord God, and that it may pleafe thee to rule and go-vern thy holy Church univerfal in the right way;

*We befeech thee to hear us, good Lord.*

That it may pleafe thee to keep and ftrengthen in the true worfhipping of thee, in righteoufnefs and holinefs of life, thy fervants the Supreme Rulers of thefe United States;

*We befeech thee to hear us, good Lord.*

That it may pleafe thee to rule their hearts in thy faith, fear, and love, that they may evermore

have

have affiance in thee, and ever feek thy honour and glory ;

*We befeech thee to hear us, good Lord.*

That it may pleafe thee to illuminate all the Minifters of thy Gofpel, with true knowledge and underftanding of thy Word : that both by their preaching and living they may fet it forth, and fhew it accordingly ;

*We befeech thee to hear us, good Lord.*

That it may pleafe thee to blefs and keep the Magiftrates, giving them grace to execute juftice, and to maintain truth ;

*We befeech thee to hear us, good Lord.*

That it may pleafe thee to blefs and keep all thy people ;

*We befeech thee to hear us, good Lord.*

That it may pleafe thee to give to all nations unity, peace and concord ;

*We befeech thee to hear us, good Lord.*

That it may pleafe thee to give us an heart to love and dread thee, and diligently to live after thy commandments ;

*We befeech thee to hear us, good Lord.*

That it may pleafe thee to give to all thy people increafe of grace, to hear meekly thy Word, and to receive it with pure affection, and to bring forth the fruits of the Spirit ;

*We befeech thee to hear us, good Lord.*

That it may pleafe thee to bring into the way of truth all fuch as have erred, and are deceived ;

*We befeech thee to hear us, good Lord.*

That it may pleafe thee to ftrengthen fuch as do ftand, and to comfort and help the weak-hearted, and to raife up them that fall, and finally to beat down Satan under our feet ;

*We befeech thee to hear us, good Lord.*

That it may pleafe thee to fuccour, help, and
comfort

comfort all that are in danger, neceffity, and tribulation ;

*We befeech thee to hear us, good Lord.*

That it may pleafe thee to preferve all that travel by land or by water, all women labouring with child, all fick perfons and young children, and to fhew thy pity upon all prifoners and captives ;

*We befeech thee to hear us, good Lord.*

That it may pleafe thee to defend, and provide for, the fatherlefs children, and widows, and all that are defolate and oppreffed ;

*We befeech thee to hear us, good Lord.*

That it may pleafe thee to have mercy upon all men ;

*We befeech thee to hear us, good Lord.*

That it may pleafe thee to forgive our enemies, perfecutors, and flanderers, and to turn their hearts ;

*We befeech thee to hear us, good Lord.*

That it may pleafe thee to give and preferve to our ufe the kindly fruits of the earth, fo as in due time we may enjoy them ;

*We befeech thee to hear us, good Lord.*

That it may pleafe thee to give us true repentance, to forgive us all our fins, negligences, and ignorances, and to endue us with the grace of thy Holy Spirit, to amend our lives according to thy holy Word ;

*We befeech thee to hear us, good Lord.*

Son of God : we befeech thee to hear us.

*Son of God : we befeech thee to hear us.*

O Lamb of God, that takeft away the fins of the world ;

*Grant us thy peace.*

O Lamb of God, that takeft away the fins of the world ;

*Have mercy upon us.*

O Chrift,

O Chrift, hear us.

> *O Chrift, hear us.*

Lord, have mercy upon us.

> *Lord, have mercy upon us.*

Chrift, have mercy upon us.

> *Chrift, have mercy upon us.*

Lord, have mercy upon us.

> *Lord, have mercy upon us.*

*Then fhall the Minifter and the People with him, fay the Lord's Prayer.*

OUR Father, who art in Heaven, Hallowed be thy Name; Thy Kingdom come; Thy will be done on earth, as it is in heaven; Give us this day our daily bread; And forgive us our trefpaffes, as we forgive them that trefpafs againft us; And lead us not into Temptation, but deliver us from evil. Amen.

*Minifter.* O Lord, deal not with us after our fins:

*Anfwer.* Neither reward us after our iniquities.

### Let us pray.

O God, merciful Father, that defpifeft not the fighing of a contrite heart, nor the defire of fuch as be forrowful; Mercifully affift our prayers that we make before thee, in all our troubles and adverfities whenfoever they opprefs us; and gracioufly hear us, that thofe evils, which the craft and fubtilty of the devil or man worketh againft us, be brought to nought, and by the providence of thy goodnefs be difperfed; that we thy fervants, being hurt by no perfecutions, may evermore give thanks unto thee in thy holy Church, through Jefus Chrift our Lord.

*O Lord, arife, help us, and deliver us for thy Name's fake.*

O God,

O God, we have heard with our Ears, and our fathers have declared unto us the noble works that thou didſt in their days, and in the old time before them.

*O Lord, ariſe, help us, and deliver us for thine honour.*

Glory be to the Father, and to the Son, and to the Holy Ghoſt.

*Anſw.* As it was in the beginning, is now, and ever ſhall be, world without end. Amen.

From our enemies defend us, O Chriſt.

*Gracioufly look upon our afflictions.*

Pitifully behold the ſorrows of our hearts.

*Mercifully forgive the ſins of thy people.*

Favourably with mercy hear our prayers.

*O Son of David, have mercy upon us.*

Both now and ever vouchſafe to hear us, O Chriſt.

*Gracioufly hear us, O Chriſt ; gracioufly hear us, O Lord Chriſt.*

O Lord, let thy mercy be ſhewed upon us ;

*As we do put our truſt in thee.*

Let us pray.

WE humbly beſeech thee, O Father, mercifully to look upon our infirmities ; and, for the glory of thy Name, turn from us all thoſe evils that we moſt righteouſly have deſerved ; and grant that in all our troubles we may put our whole truſt and confidence in thy mercy, and evermore ſerve thee in holineſs and pureneſs of living, to thy honour and glory, through our only Mediator and Advocate, Jeſus Chriſt our Lord. *Amen.*

ALmighty God, who haſt given us grace at this time with one accord to make our common ſupplications unto thee, and doſt promiſe that when two or three are gathered together in thy Name, thou wilt grant their requeſts ; fulfil now, O Lord, the defires and petitions of thy fervants, as may be moft expedient for them : granting us in this world knowledge of thy truth, and in the world to come life everlafting. *Amen.*

### 2 *Cor.* xiii. 14.

THE grace of our Lord, Jefus Chrift, and the love of God, and the fellowfhip of the Holy Ghoft, be with you all evermore. *Amen.*

*Here endeth the LITANY.*

---

## A PRAYER *and* THANKSGIVING, *to be ufed every Lord's Day.*

O God, the Creator and Preferver of all man-kind, we humbly befeech thee for all forts and conditions of men, that thou wouldeft be pleafed to make thy ways known unto them, thy faving health unto all nations. More efpecially we pray for the good eftate of the Catholic Church ; that it may be fo guided and governed by thy good Spirit, that all who profefs and call themfelves Chriftians may be led into the way of truth, and hold the faith in unity of fpirit, in the bond of peace, and in righteoufnefs of life. Finally, we commend to thy fatherly goodnefs, all thofe who are any ways afflicted or dif-treffed in mind, body, or eftate [* *efpe-cially thofe for whom our prayers are de-fired*]; that it may pleafe thee to comfort and relieve them according to their feveral neceffities ; giving them patience under their fufferings, and a happy iffue out of all their afflictions : and this we beg for Jefus Chrift's fake. *Amen.*

* *This to be faid when any defire the prayers of the Congrega-tion.*

Almighty

## A General Thankſgiving.

ALmighty God, Father of all mercies, we thine unworthy ſervants do give thee moſt humble and hearty thanks for all thy goodneſs and loving-kindneſs to us and to all men; [* *particularly to thoſe who deſire now to offer up their praiſes and thankſgivings for thy late mercies vouchſafed unto them.*] We bleſs thee for our creation, preſervation, and all the bleſſings of this life; but above all, for thine ineſtimable love in the redemption of the world by our Lord Jeſus Chriſt; for the means of grace, and for the hope of glory. And we beſeech thee, give us that due ſenſe of all thy mercies, that our hearts may be unfeignedly thankful, and that we may ſhew forth thy praiſe not only with our lips, but in our lives, by giving up ourſelves to thy ſervice, and by walking before thee in holineſs and righteouſneſs all our days, through Jeſus Chriſt our Lord, to whom with thee and the Holy Ghoſt, be all honour and glory, world without end. *Amen.*

*\* This to be ſaid when any that have been prayed for deſire to return praiſe.*

THE

# COLLECTS, EPISTLES, and GOSPELS,

To be ufed throughout the Year.

*The Firft Sunday in Advent.*

*The Colleƈt.*

ALmighty God, give us grace that we may caft away the works of darknefs, and put upon us the armour of light, now in the time of this mortal life, in which thy Son Jefus Chrift came to vifit us in great humility; that in the laft day, when he fhall come again in his glorious Majefty, to judge both the quick and dead, we may rife to the life immortal, through him who liveth and reigneth with thee and the Holy Ghoft, now and ever. *Amen.*

*Epistle:* Romans 13:8-14  *Gospel:* Matthew 21:1-13

*The Second Sunday in Advent.*

*The Colleƈt.*

BLefed Lord, who haft caufed all holy Scriptures to be written for our learning; Grant th.t we may in fuch wife hear them, read, mark, learn, and inwardly digeft them, that by patience and comfort of thy holy word, we may embrace and ever hold faft the bleff d hope of everlafting life, which thou haft given us in our Saviour Jefus Chrift. *Amen.*

*Epistle:* Romans 15:4-13  *Gospel:* Luke 21:25-33

[27-31]

*The Third Sunday in Advent.*
*The Collect.*

O Lord Jesus Christ, who at thy first coming didst send thy messenger to prepare thy way before thee, grant that the ministers and stewards of thy mysteries may likewise so prepare and make ready thy way, by turning the hearts of the disobedient to the wisdom of the just, that at thy second coming to judge the world, we may be found an acceptable people in thy sight, who liveft and reigneft with the Father and the Holy Spirit, ever one God, world without end. *Amen.*

*Epistle:* 1 Corinthians 4:1-5       *Gospel:* Matthew 11:2-10

*The Fourth Sunday in Advent.*
*The Collect.*

O Lord, raise up, we pray thee, thy power, and come among us, and with great might succour us ; that whereas, through our sins and wickedness, we are sore let and hindered in running the race that is set before us, thy bountiful grace and mercy may speedily help and deliver us, through the satisfaction of thy Son our Lord ; to whom with thee and the Holy Ghost be honour and glory, world without end. *Amen.*

*Epistle:* Philippians 4:4-7       *Gospel:* John 1:19-28

[31-33]

*The Nativity of our Lord, or the Birth-day of CHRIST, commonly called* Chriftmas-day.

*The Collect.*

ALmighty God, who haft given us thy only begotten Son to take our nature upon him, and as at this Time to be born of a pure Virgin, grant that we, being regenerate, and made thy children by adoption and grace, may daily be renewed by thy Holy Spirit, through the fame our Lord Jefus Chrift, who liveth and reigneth with thee and the fame Spirit, ever one God, world without end. *Amen.*

*Epistle:* Hebrews 1:1-12          *Gospel:* John 1:1-14

*The Firft Sunday after Chriftmas.*

*The Collect.*

ALmighty God, who haft given us thy only begotten Son to take our nature upon him, and as at this time to be born of a pure Virgin ; grant that we, being regenerate and made thy children by adoption and grace, may daily be renewed by thy Holy Spirit, through the fame our Lord Jefus Chrift, who liveth and reigneth with thee and the fame Spirit, ever one God, world without end. *Amen.*

*Epistle:* Galatians 4:1-7          *Gospel:* Matthew 1:18-25

*The Second Sunday after Chriftmas.*

*The Collect.*

O Lord, we befeech thee, mercifully to receive the prayers of thy people who call upon thee ; and grant that they may both perceive and know what things they ought to do, and alfo may have grace and power faithfully to fulfil the fame, through Jefus Chrift our Lord. Amen.

*Epistle:* Romans 12:1-5          *Gospel:* Luke 2:41-52

[33-38]

*The Third Sunday after Chriſtmas.*

*The Collect.*

A Lmighty and everlaſting God, who doſt govern all things in heaven and earth; Mercifully hear the ſupplications of thy people, and grant us thy peace all the days of our life, through Jeſus Chriſt our Lord. *Amen.*

*Epistle:* Romans 12:6-16b          *Gospel:* John 2:1-11

*The Fourth Sunday after Chriſtmas.*

*The Collect.*

A Lmighty and everlaſting God, mercifully look upon our infirmities, and in all our dangers and neceſſities ſtretch forth thy right hand to help and defend us, through Jeſus Chriſt our Lord. *Amen.*

*Epistle:* Romans 12:16c-21          *Gospel:* Matthew 8:1-13

*The Fifth Sunday after Chriſtmas.*

*The Collect.*

O God, who knoweſt us to be ſet in the midſt of ſo many and great dangers, that by reaſon of the frailty of our nature we cannot always ſtand upright, grant to us ſuch ſtrength and protection as may ſupport us in all dangers, and carry us through all temptations, through Jeſus Chriſt our Lord. *Amen.*

*Epistle:* Romans 13:1-7          *Gospel:* Matthew 8:23-34

*The Sixth Sunday after Chriſtmas.*

*The Collect.*

O Lord, we beſeech thee to keep thy church and houſhold continually in thy true religion; that they, who do lean only upon the hope of thy heavenly grace, may evermore be defended by thy mighty power, through Jeſus Chriſt our Lord. *Amen.*

*Epistle:* Colossians 3:12-17          *Gospel:* Matthew 13:24b-30

[38-44]

*The Seventh Sunday after Chriſtmas.*

*The Collect.*

O God, whoſe bleſſed Son was manifeſted, that he might deſtroy the works of the devil, and make us the ſons of God, and heirs of eternal life; Grant us, we beſeech thee, that having this

hope, we may purify ourſelves even as he is pure; that when he ſhall appear again with power and great glory, we may be made like unto him in his eternal and glorious kingdom; where with thee, O Father, and thee, O Holy Ghoſt, he liveth and reigneth, ever one God, world without end. *Amen.*

*Epistle:* 1 John 3:1-8          *Gospel:* Matthew 24:23-31

*The Eighth Sunday after Chriſtmas.*

*The Collect.*

O Lord, we beſeech thee, favourably to hear the prayers of thy people; that we who are juſtly puniſhed for our offences, may be mercifully delivered by thy goodneſs, for the glory of thy Name, through Jeſus Chriſt our Saviour, who liveth and reigneth with thee and the Holy Ghoſt, ever one God, world without end. *Amen.*

*Epistle:* 1 Corinthians 9:24-27          *Gospel:* Matthew 20:1-16

*The Ninth Sunday after Chriſtmas.*

*The Ninth Sunday after Chriſtmas.*

*The Collect.*

O Lord God, who ſeeſt that we put not our truſt in any thing that we do; Mercifully grant that by thy power we may be defended againſt all adverſity, through Jeſus Chriſt our Lord. *Amen.*

*Epistle:* 2 Corinthians 11:19-31          *Gospel:* Luke 8:14-15

[44-49]

### The Tenth Sunday after Chriſtmas.
#### The Collect.

O Lord, who haſt taught us, that all our doings without love are nothing worth ; ſend thy Holy Spirit, and pour into our hearts that moſt excellent gift of love, the very bond of peace, and of all virtues ; without which whoſoever liveth is counted dead before thee. Grant this for thine only Son Jeſus Chriſt s ſake. *Amen.*

*Epistle:* 2 Corinthians 13:1-13          *Gospel:* Luke 18:31-43

### The Eleventh Sunday after Chriſtmas.
#### The Collect.

O Lord, who for our ſake didſt faſt forty days and forty nights ; give us grace to uſe ſuch abſtinence, that our fleſh being ſubdued to the Spirit, we may ever obey thy godly motions in righteouſneſs and true holineſs, to thy honour and glory, who liveſt and reigneſt with the Father and the Holy Ghoſt, one God, world without end. *Amen.*

*Epistle:* 2 Corinthians 6:1-10          *Gospel:* Matthew 4:1-11

### The Twelfth Sunday after Chriſtmas.
#### The Collect.

A Lmighty God, who ſeeſt that we have no power of ourſelves to help ourſelves ; Keep us both outwardly in our bodies, and inwardly in our ſouls, that we may be defended from all adverſities which may happen to the body, and from all evil thoughts which may aſſault and hurt the ſoul, through Jeſus Chriſt our Lord. *Amen.*

*Epistle:* 1 Thessalonians 4:1-8          *Gospel:* Matthew 15:21-28

[50-54]

*The Thirteenth Sunday after Chriſtmas.*

*The Collect.*

WE beſeech thee, Almighty God, look upon the hearty deſires of thy humble ſervants, and ſtretch forth the right hand of thy Majeſty to be our defence againſt all our enemies, through Jeſus Chriſt our Lord. *Amen.*

*Epistle:* Ephesians 5:1-14          *Gospel:* Luke 11:14-28

*The Fourteenth Sunday after Chriſtmas.*

*The Collect.*

GRant, we beſeech thee, Almighty God, that we who, for our evil deeds do worthily deſerve to be puniſhed, by the comfort of thy grace may mercifully be relieved, through our Lord and Saviour Jeſus Chriſt. *Amen.*

*Epistle:* Galatians 4:21-31          *Gospel:* John 6:1-14

*The Fifteenth Sunday after Chriſtmas.*

*The Collect.*

WE beſeech thee, Almighty God, mercifully to look upon thy people; that by thy great goodneſs they may be governed and preſerved evermore, both in body and ſoul, through Jeſus Chriſt our Lord. *Amen.*

*Epistle:* Hebrews 9:11-15          *Gospel:* John 8:46-59

*The Sunday next before Easter.*

*The Collect.*

ALmighty and everlasting God, who of thy tender love towards mankind, hast sent thy Son our Saviour Jesus Christ, to take upon him our flesh, and to suffer death upon the cross, that all mankind should follow the example of his great humility; Mercifully grant, that we may both follow the example of his patience, and also be made partakers of his resurrection, through the same Jesus Christ our Lord. *Amen.*

*Epistle:* Philippians 2:5-11        *Gospel:* Matthew 27:1-54

## GOOD-FRIDAY.

*The Collects.*

ALmighty God, we beseech thee graciously to behold this thy family, for which our Lord Jesus Christ was contented to be betrayed, and given up into the hands of wicked men, and to suffer death upon the cross, who now liveth and reigneth with thee and the Holy Ghost, ever one God, world without end. *Amen.*

ALmighty and everlasting God, by whose Spirit the whole body of the Church is governed and sanctified; Receive our supplications and prayers which we offer before thee for all estates of men in thy holy Church, that every member of the same, in his vocation and ministry, may truly and godly serve thee, through our Lord and Saviour Jesus Christ. *Amen.*

O Merciful God, who haſt made all men, and hateſt nothing that thou haſt made, nor wouldeſt the death of a ſinner, but rather that he ſhould be converted, and live ; Have mercy upon all Jews, Turks, Infidels, and Heretics, and take from them all ignorance, hardneſs of heart, and contempt of thy Word; and ſo fetch them home, bleſſed Lord, to thy flock, that they may be ſaved among the remnant of the true Iſraelites, and be made one fold under one Shepherd, Jeſus Chriſt our Lord, who liveth and reigneth with thee and the Holy Spirit, One God, world without end. *Amen.*

*Epistle:* Hebrews 10:1-25          *Gospel:* John 19:1-37

## EASTER-DAY.

*At Morning Prayer, before the Pſalms, theſe Anthems ſhall be ſaid.*

CHRIST our paſſover is ſacrificed for us ; therefore let us keep the feaſt ;

Not with the old leaven, neither with the leaven of malice and wickedneſs, but with the unleavened bread of ſincerity and truth. 1 *Cor.* v. 7.

CHRIST being raiſed from the dead, dieth no more: death hath no more dominion over him.

For in that he died, he died unto ſin once ; but in that he liveth, he liveth unto God.

Likewiſe reckon ye alſo yourſelves to be dead indeed unto ſin, but alive unto God, through Jeſus Chriſt our Lord. *Rom.* vi. 9.

CHRIST is riſen from the dead, and become the firſt-fruits of them that ſlept.

For ſince by man came death, by man came alſo the reſurrection of the dead.

For as in Adam all die, even ſo in Chriſt ſhall all be made alive. 1 *Cor.* xv. 20.

Glory be to the Father, and to the Son, and to the Holy Ghoſt ;

*Anſw.* As it was in the beginning, is now, and ever ſhall be, world without end. *Amen.*

[65-70]

*The Collect.*

ALmighty God, who, through thine only-begotten Son Jefus Chrift, haft overcome death, and opened unto us the gate of everlafting life, we humbly befeech thee, that, as by thy fpecial grace preventing us, thou doft put into our minds good defires; fo by thy continual help we may bring the fame to good effect, through Jefus Chrift our Lord, who liveth and reigneth with thee and the Holy Ghoft, ever one God, world without end. *Amen.*

*Epistle:* Colossians 3:1-7          *Gospel:* John 20:1-10

*The Firft Sunday after Eafter.*

*The Collect.*

ALmighty Father, who haft given thine only Son to die for our fins, and to rife again for our juftification, grant us fo to put away the leaven of malice and wickednefs, that we may alway ferve thee in purenefs of living and truth, through the merits of the fame thy Son Jefus Chrift our Lord. *Amen.*

*Epistle:* 1 John 5:4-12          *Gospel:* John 20:19-23

[70-73]

### The Second Sunday after Eafter.

#### The Collect.

ALmighty God, who haft given thine only Son to be unto us both a facrifice for fin, and alfo an enfample of godly life, give us grace, that we may always moft thankfully receive that his ineftimable benefit ; and alfo daily endeavour ourfelves to follow the bleffed fteps of his moft holy life, through the fame Jefus Chrift our Lord. *Amen.*

*Epistle:* 1 Peter 2:19-25          *Gospel:* John 10:11-16

### The Third Sunday after Eafter.

#### The Collect.

ALmighty God, who fheweft to them that are in error the light of thy truth, to the intent that they may return into the way of righteoufnefs, grant unto all them that are admitted into the fellowfhip of Chrift's religion, that they may efchew thofe things that are contrary to their profeffion, and follow all fuch things as are agreeable to the fame, through our Lord Jefus Chrift. *Amen.*

*Epistle:* 1 Peter 2:11-17          *Gospel:* John 16:16-24

### The Fourth Sunday after Eafter.

#### The Collect.

O Almighty God, who alone canft order the unruly wills and affections of finful men, grant unto thy people, that they may love the thing which thou commandeft, and defire that which thou doft promife ; that fo among the fundry and manifold changes of the world, our hearts may furely there be fixed, where true joys are to be found, through Jefus Chrift our Lord. *Amen.*

*Epistle:* James 1:17-21          *Gospel:* John 16:5-15

[73-77]

*The Fifth Sunday after Eafter.*

*The Collect.*

O Lord, from whom all good things do come, grant to us thy humble fervants, that, by thy holy infpiration, we may think thofe things that are good, and, by thy merciful guiding, may perform the fame, through our Lord Jefus Chrift. *Amen.*

*Epistle:* James 1:22-27          *Gospel:* John 16:23b-33

*The Afcenfion-day.*

*The Collect.*

GRANT, we befeech thee, Almighty God, that like as we do believe thy only-begotten Son our Lord Jefus Chrift to have afcended into the heavens, fo we may alfo in heart and mind thither afcend, and with him continually dwell, who liveth and reigneth with thee and the Holy Ghoft, one God, world without end. *Amen.*

*For the Epistle:* Acts 1:1-11          *Gospel:* Mark 16:14-21

*Sunday after Afcenfion-day.*

*The Collect.*

O God, the King of glory, who haft exalted thine only Son Jefus Chrift with great triumph unto thy kingdom in heaven, we befeech thee leave us not comfortlefs, but fend to us thine Holy Ghoft to comfort us, and exalt us unto the fame place whither our Saviour Chrift is gone before; who liveth and reigneth with thee and the Holy Ghoft, one God, world without end. *Amen.*

*Epistle:* 1 Peter 4:7-11          *Gospel:* John 15:26-16:4

## WHIT-SUNDAY.

### *The Collect.*

O God, who as at this time didst teach the hearts of thy faithful people, by the sending to them the light of thy holy Spirit; Grant us by the same Spirit to have a right judgment in all things, and evermore to rejoice in his holy comfort, through the merits of Christ Jesus our Saviour, who liveth and reigneth with thee, in the unity of the same Spirit, one God, world without end. *Amen.*

*For the Epistle:* Acts 2:1-11    *Gospel:* John 14:15-31b

## TRINITY-SUNDAY.

### *The Collect.*

A Lmighty and everlasting God, who hast given unto us thy servants grace, by the confession of a true Faith, to acknowledge the glory of the eternal Trinity, and in the power of the Divine Majesty to worship the Unity; We beseech thee, that thou wouldst keep us stedfast in this faith, and evermore defend us from all adversities, who livest and reignest, one God, world without end. *Amen.*

*For the Epistle:* Revelation 4:1-11    *Gospel:* John 3:1-15

### *The First Sunday after Trinity.*
### *The Collect.*

O God, the strength of all them that put their trust in thee, mercifully accept our prayers; and because through the weakness of our mortal nature we can do no good thing without thee, grant us the help of thy grace, that in keeping thy commandments, we may please thee both in will and deed, through Jesus Christ our Lord. *Amen.*

*Epistle:* 1 John 4:7-21    *Gospel:* Luke 16:19-31

[82-88]

### The Second Sunday after Trinity.

#### The Collect.

O LORD, who never faileft to help, and govern them whom thou doft bring up in thy ftedfaft fear and love; Keep us, we befeech thee, under the protection of thy good providence, and make us to have a perpetual fear and love of thy holy Name, through Jefus Chrift our Lord. *Amen.*

*Epistle:* 1 John 3:13-24          *Gospel:* Luke 14:16-24

### The third Sunday after Trinity.

#### The Collect.

O LORD, we befeech thee mercifully to hear us; and grant that we, to whom thou haft given an hearty defire to pray, may by thy mighty aid be defended and comforted in all dangers and adverfities, through Jefus Chrift our Lord. *Amen.*

*Epistle:* 1 Peter 5:5b-11          *Gospel:* Luke 15:1-10

### The Fourth Sunday after Trinity.

#### The Collect.

O God, the protector of all that truft in thee, without whom nothing is ftrong, nothing is holy; Increafe and multiply upon us thy mercy, that thou being our ruler and guide, we may fo pafs through things temporal, that we finally lofe not the things eternal: Grant this, O heavenly Father, for Jefus Chrift's fake our Lord. *Amen.*

*Epistle:* Romans 8:18-23          *Gospel:* Luke 6:36-42

[89-93]

*The Fifth Sunday after Trinity.*

*The Colleĉt.*

GRANT, O Lord, we befeech thee, that the courfe of this world may be fo peaceably ordered by thy governance, that thy Church may joyfully ferve thee in all godly quietnefs, through Jefus Chrift our Lord. *Amen.*

*Epistle:* 1 Peter 3:8-15a          *Gospel:* Luke 5:1-11

*The Sixth Sunday after Trinity.*

*The Colleĉt.*

O God, who haft prepared for them that love thee, fuch good things as pafs man's underftanding; pour into our hearts fuch love toward thee, that we loving thee above all things, may obtain thy promifes, which exceed all that we can defire, through Jefus Chrift our Lord. *Amen.*

*Epistle:* Romans 6:3-11          *Gospel:* Matthew 5:20-26

*The Seventh Sunday after Trinity.*

*The Colleĉt.*

LORD of all power and might, who art the author and giver of all good things; graft in our hearts the love of thy name, increafe in us true religion, nourifh us with all goodnefs, and of thy great mercy keep us in the fame, through Jefus Chrift our Lord. *Amen.*

*Epistle:* Romans 6:19-23          *Gospel:* Mark 8:1-9

[93-97]

### *The Eighth Sunday after Trinity.*
#### *The Collect.*

O God, whofe never-failing providence ordereth all things both in heaven and earth; we humbly befeech thee to put away from us all hurtful things, and to give us thofe things which are profitable for us, through Jefus Chrift our Lord. *Amen.*

*Epistle:* Romans 8:12-17          *Gospel:* Matthew 7:15-21

### *The Ninth Sunday after Trinity.*
#### *The Collect.*

GRANT to us, Lord, we befeech thee, the fpirit to think and do always fuch things as be rightful; that we, who cannot do any thing that is good without thee, may by thee be enabled to live according to thy will, through Jefus Chrift our Lord. *Amen.*

*Epistle:* 1 Corinthians 10:1-13          *Gospel:* Luke 16:1-9

### *The Tenth Sunday after Trinity.*
#### *The Collect.*

LET thy merciful ears, O Lord, be open to the prayers of thy humble fervants; and that they may obtain their petitions, make them to

afk fuch things as fhall pleafe thee, through Jefus Cnrift our Lord. *Amen.*

*Epistle:* 1 Corinthians 12:1-11          *Gospel:* Luke 19:41-47a

[98-102]

*The Eleventh Sunday after Trinity.*

*The Collect.*

O God, who declareft thy almighty power moft chiefly in fhewing mercy and pity ; mercifully grant unto us fuch a meafure of thy grace, that we running the way of thy commandments, may obtain thy gracious promifes, and be made partakers of thy heavenly treafure, through Jefus Chrift our Lord. *Amen.*

*Epistle:* 1 Corinthians 15:1-11       *Gospel:* Luke 18:9-14

*The Twelfth Sunday after Trinity.*

*The Collect.*

ALmighty and everlafting God, who art always more ready to hear than we to pray, and art wont to give more than either we defire or deferve, pour down upon us the abundance of thy mercy, forgiving us thofe things whereof our confcience is afraid, and giving us thofe good things which we are not worthy to afk, but through the merits and mediation of Jefus Chrift thy Son, our Lord. *Amen.*

*Epistle:* 2 Corinthians 3:4-8       *Gospel:* Mark 7:31-37

*The Thirteenth Sunday after Trinity.*

*The Collect.*

ALmighty and merciful God, of whofe only gift it cometh that thy faithful people do unto thee true and laudable fervice, grant, we befeech thee, that we may fo faithfully ferve thee in this life, that we fail not finally to attain thy heavenly promifes, through the merits of Jefus Chrift our Lord. *Amen.*

*Epistle:* Galatians 3:16-22       *Gospel:* Luke 10:23-37

[102-106]

*The Fourteenth Sunday after Trinity.*

*The Collect.*

ALmighty and everlasting God, give unto us the increase of faith, hope, and love ; and that we may obtain that which thou dost promise, make us to love that which thou dost command, through Jesus Christ our Lord. *Amen.*

*Epistle:* Galatians 5:16-24        *Gospel:* Luke 17:11-19

*The Fifteenth Sunday after Trinity.*

*The Collect.*

KEEP, we beseech thee, O Lord, thy church with thy perpetual mercy ; and, because the frailty of man without thee cannot but fall, keep us ever by thy help from all things hurtful, and lead us to all things profitable to our salvation, through Jesus Christ our Lord. *Amen.*

*Epistle:* Galatians 6:11-18        *Gospel:* Matthew 6:24-34

*The Sixteenth Sunday after Trinity.*

*The Collect.*

O Lord, we beseech thee, let thy continual pity cleanse and defend thy Church ; and because it cannot continue in safety without thy succour, preserve it evermore by thy help and goodness, through Jesus Christ our Lord. *Amen.*

Epistle: Ephesians 3:13-21        Gospel: Luke 7:11-17

*The Seventeenth Sunday after Trinity.*

*The Collect.*

LORD, we pray thee, that thy grace may always prevent and follow us ; and make us continually to be given to all good works, through Jesus Christ our Lord. *Amen.*

*Epistle:* Ephesians 4:1-6        *Gospel:* Luke 14:1-11

*The Eighteenth Sunday after Trinity.*

*The Collect.*

LOrd, we befeech thee, grant thy people grace to withftand the temptations of the world, the flefh, and the devil, and with pure hearts and minds to follow thee, the only God, through Jefus Chrift our Lord. *Amen.*

*Epistle:* 1 Corinthians 1:4-8      *Gospel:* Matthew 22:34-46

*The Nineteenth Sunday after Trinity.*

*The Collect.*

O God, forafmuch as without thee we are not able to pleafe thee ; Mercifully grant, that thy Holy Spirit may in all things direct and rule our hearts, through Jefus Chrift our Lord. *Amen.*

*Epistle:* Ephesians 4:17-32      *Gospel:* Matthew 9:1-8

*The Twentieth Sunday after Trinity.*

*The Collect.*

O Almighty and moft merciful God, of thy bountiful goodnefs keep us, we befeech thee, from all things that may hurt us ; that we being ready both in body and foul, may chearfully accomplifh thofe things that thou wouldeft have done, through Jefus Chrift our Lord. *Amen.*

*Epistle:* Ephesians 5:15-21      *Gospel:* Matthew 22:1-14

*The Twenty-firft Sunday after Trinity.*

*The Collect.*

GRANT, we befeech thee, merciful Lord, to thy faithful people pardon and peace ; that they may be cleanfed from all their fins, and ferve thee with a quiet mind, through Jefus Chrift our Lord. *Amen.*

*Epistle:* Ephesians 6:10-20      *Gospel:* John 4:46b-54

*The Twenty-second Sunday after Trinity.*

*The Collect.*

L ORD, we beseech thee to keep thy houshold the Church in continual godliness ; that through thy protection it may be free from all adversities, and devoutly given to serve thee in good works, to the glory of thy name, through Jesus Christ our Lord. *Amen.*

*Epistle:* Philippians 1:3-11          *Gospel:* Matthew 18:21-35

*The Twenty-third Sunday after Trinity.*

*The Collect.*

O God, our refuge and strength, who art the author of all godliness ; be ready, we beseech thee, to hear the devout prayers of thy Church ; and grant that those things which we ask faithfully, we may obtain effectually, through Jesus Christ our Lord. *Amen.*

*Epistle:* Philippians 3:17-21          *Gospel:* Matthew 22:15-22

*The Twenty-fourth Sunday after Trinity.*

*The Collect.*

O LORD, we beseech thee, absolve thy people from their offences ; that through thy bountiful goodness we may all be delivered from the bands of those sins, which by our frailty we have committed.   Grant this, O heavenly Father, for Jesus Christ's sake, our blessed Lord and Saviour. *Amen.*

*Epistle:* Colossians 1:3-12          *Gospel:* Matthew 9:18-26

[118-123]

*The Twenty fifth Sunday after Trinity.*

*The Colle&.*

STIR up, we befeech thee, O Lord, the wills of thy faithful people ; that they plenteoufly bringing forth the fruit of good works, may of thee be plenteoufly rewarded, through Jefus Chrift our Lord. *Amen.*

*For the Epistle:* Jeremiah 23:5-8      *Gospel:* John 6:5-14

# The Order for the Adminiſtration of the Lord's Supper.

*The Table at the Communion-time, having a fair white Linen Cloth upon it, ſhall ſtand where Morning and Evening Prayers are appointed to be ſaid. And the Elder, ſtanding at the Table, ſhall ſay the Lord's Prayer, with the Collect following, the People kneeling.*

OUR Father, who art in Heaven, Hallowed be thy Name; Thy Kingdom come; Thy will be done on earth, as it is in heaven; Give us this day our daily bread; And forgive us our treſpaſſes, as we forgive them that treſpaſs againſt us; And lead us not into Temptation, but deliver us from evil. *Amen.*

## The Collect.

ALmighty God, unto whom all hearts be open, all deſires known, and from whom no ſecrets are hid; cleanſe the thoughts of our hearts by the inſpiration of thy Holy Spirit, that we may perfectly love thee, and worthily magnify thy holy Name, through Chriſt our Lord. *Amen.*

*Then ſhall the Elder, turning to the People, rehearſe diſtinctly all the TEN COMMANDMENTS: and the People ſtill kneeling ſhall, after every Commandment, aſk God Mercy for their Tranſgreſſion thereof for the Time paſt, and Grace to keep the ſame for the Time to come, as followeth :*

## Miniſter.

GOD ſpake theſe words, and ſaid, I am the Lord thy God: Thou ſhalt have none other gods but me.

People.

*People.* Lord, have mercy upon us, and incline our hearts to keep this law.

*Minift.* Thou fhalt not make to thyfelf any graven image, nor the likenefs of any thing that is in heaven above, or in the earth beneath, or in the water under the earth. Thou fhalt not bow down to them, nor worfhip them: for I the Lord thy God am a jealous God, and vifit the fins of the fathers upon the children, unto the third and fourth generation of them that hate me, and fhew mercy unto thoufands in them that love me, and keep my commandments.

*People.* Lord, have mercy upon us, and incline our hearts to keep this law.

*Minift.* Thou fhalt not take the Name of the Lord thy God in vain: for the Lord will not hold him guiltlefs that taketh his Name in vain.

*People.* Lord, have mercy upon us, and incline our hearts to keep this law.

*Minift.* Remember that thou keep holy the Sabbath-day. Six days fhalt thou labour, and do all that thou haft to do; but the feventh day is the Sabbath of the Lord thy God: in it thou fhalt do no manner of work, thou, and thy fon, and thy daughter, thy man-fervant, and thy maid-fervant, thy cattle, and the ftranger that is within thy gates. For in fix days the Lord made heaven and earth, the fea, and all that in them is, and refted the feventh day; wherefore the Lord bleffed the feventh day, and hallowed it.

*People.* Lord, have mercy upon us, and incline our hearts to keep this law.

*Minift.* Honour thy father and thy mother, that thy days may be long in the land which the Lord thy God giveth thee.

*People.* Lord, have mercy upon us, and incline our hearts to keep this law.

*Minift.*

*Minist.* Thou shalt do no murder.

*People.* Lord, have mercy upon us, and incline our hearts to keep this law.

*Minist.* Thou shalt not commit adultery.

*People.* Lord, have mercy upon us, and incline our hearts to keep this law.

*Minist.* Thou shalt not steal.

*People.* Lord, have mercy upon us, and incline our hearts to keep this law.

*Minist.* Thou shalt not bear false witness against thy neighbour.

*People.* Lord, have mercy upon us, and incline our hearts to keep this law.

*Minist.* Thou shalt not covet thy neighbour's house, thou shalt not covet thy neighbour's wife, nor his servant, nor his maid, nor his ox, nor his ass, nor any thing that is his.

*People.* Lord, have mercy upon us, and write all these thy laws in our hearts, we beseech thee.

*Then shall follow this Collect.*

### Let us pray.

ALmighty and everlasting God, we are taught by thy holy word, that the hearts of the Princes of the earth are in thy rule and governance, and that thou dost dispose and turn them as it seemeth best to thy godly wisdom ; we humbly beseech thee so to dispose and govern the hearts of the Supreme Rulers of these United States, our Governors, that in all their thoughts, words, and works, they may ever seek thy honour and glory, and study to preserve thy people committed to their charge, in wealth, peace, and godliness. Grant this, O merciful Father, for thy dear Son's sake, Jesus Christ our Lord. *Amen.*

F 4

*Then*

*Then ſhall be ſaid the Collect of the day.　And imme-
diately after the Collect, the Elder ſhall read the
Epiſtle, ſaying,* The Epiſtle [*or,* The Portion of
Scripture appointed for the Epiſtle] is written
in the —— Chapter of —— beginning at the
—— Verſe　*And the Epiſtle ended, he ſhall ſay,*
Here endeth the Epiſtle.　*Then ſhall he read the
Goſpel, (the People all ſtanding up) ſaying,* The
holy Goſpel is written in the —— Chapter of
—— beginning at the —— Verſe.

*Then ſhall follow the Sermon.*

*Then ſhall the Elder ſay one or more of theſe Sentences.*

LET your light ſo ſhine before men, that they
may ſee your good works, and glorify your
Father who is in heaven.　*Matth.* v. 16.

Lay not up for yourſelves treaſures upon earth,
where moth and ruſt do corrupt, and where thieves
break through and ſteal : but lay up for yourſelves
treaſures in heaven, where neither moth nor ruſt
doth corrupt, and where thieves do not break
through nor ſteal.　*Matth.* vi. 19, 20.

Whatſoever ye would that men ſhould do unto
you, even ſo do unto them ; for this is the law and
the prophets.　*Matth.* vii. 12.

Not every one that ſaith unto me, Lord, Lord,
ſhall enter into the kingdom of heaven ; but he that
doeth the will of my Father who is in heaven.
*Matth.* vii. 21.

Zaccheus ſtood forth, and ſaid unto the Lord,
Behold, Lord, the half of my goods I give to the
poor ; and if I have done any wrong to any man,
I reſtore him four-fold.　*Luke,* xix. 8.

Who goeth a warfare at any time of his own
coſt ? who planteth a vineyard, and eateth not of
the fruit thereof ? or who feedeth a flock, and
eateth not of the milk of the flock ?　1 *Cor.* ix. 7.

If

If we have fown unto you fpiritual things, is it a great matter if we fhall reap your worldly things? *1 Cor.* ix. 11.

Do ye not know, that they who minifter about holy things, live of the facrifice? and they who wait at the altar, are partakers with the altar? Even fo hath the Lord alfo ordained, that they who preach the Gofpel, fhould live of the Gofpel. *1 Cor.* ix. 13, 14.

He that foweth little, fhall reap little : and he that foweth plenteoufly, fhall reap plenteoufly. Let every man do according as he is difpofed in his heart ; not grudgingly, or of neceffity : for God loveth a chearful giver. *2 Cor.* ix. 6, 7.

Let him that is taught in the Word, minifter unto him that teacheth in all good things. Be not deceived, God is not mocked: for whatfoever a man foweth, that fhall he reap. *Gal.* vi. 6, 7.

While we have time, let us do good unto all men, and efpecially unto them that are of the houfhold of faith. *Gal.* vi. 10.

Godlinefs with contentment is great gain : for we brought nothing into the world, and it is certain we can carry nothing out. *1 Tim.* vi. 6, 7.

Charge them who are rich in this world, that they be ready to give, and glad to diftribute, laying up in ftore for themfelves a good foundation againft the time to come, that they may attain eternal life. *1 Tim.* vi. 17, 18, 19.

God is not unrighteous, that he will forget your works and labour that proceedeth of love ; which love ye have fhewed for his Name's fake, who have miniftered unto the faints, and yet do minifter. *Heb.* vi. 10.

To do good, and to diftribute, forget not ; for with fuch facrifices God is well pleafed. *Hebr.* xiii. 16.

F 5 Whofo

Whofo hath this world's good, and feeth his brother have need, and fhutteth up his compaffion from him, how dwelleth the love of God in him? *1 John,* iii. 17.

Be merciful after thy power : If thou haft much, give plenteoufly : If thou haft little, do thy diligence gladly to give of that little : for fo gathereft thou thyfelf a good reward in the day of neceffity. *Tob.* iv. 8, 9.

He that hath pity upon the poor, lendeth unto the Lord ; and look what he layeth out, it fhall be paid him again. *Prov.* xix. 17.

Bleffed is the man that provideth for the fick and needy : the Lord fhall deliver him in the time of trouble. *Pfal.* xli. 1.

*While thefe Sentences are in reading, fome fit perfon appointed for that purpofe, fhall receive the alms for the poor, and other devotions of the people, in a decent Bafon, to be provided for that purpofe ; and then bring it to the Elder, who fhall place it upon the Table.*

*After which done, the Elder fhall fay,*

Let us pray for the whole ftate of Chrift's Church militant here on earth.

ALmighty and everliving God, who, by thy holy Apoftle, haft taught us to make prayers and fupplications, and to give thanks for all men ; We humbly befeech thee moft mercifully [* to accept our alms and oblations, and] to receive thefe our prayers, which we offer unto thy Divine Majefty ; befeeching thee to infpire continually the univerfal Church with the fpirit of truth, unity, and concord : and grant that all they that do confefs thy holy Name, may agree in the truth of thy holy word, and live in unity and godly love. We befeech thee

*\* If there be no alms or oblations, then fhall the words [of accepting our alms and oblations] be left unfaid.*

7
thee

thee alfo to fave and defend all Chriftian Kings, Princes, and Governors ; and efpecially thy Servants the Supreme Rulers of thefe United States ; that under them we may be godly and quietly governed : and grant unto all that are put in authority under them, that they may truly and indifferently adminifter juftice, to the punifhment of wickednefs and vice, and to the maintenance of thy true religion and virtue. Give grace, O heavenly Father, to all the Minifters of thy Gofpel, that they may both by their life and doctrine fet forth thy true and lively word, and rightly and duly adminifter thy holy Sacraments. And to all thy people give thy heavenly grace ; and efpecially to this Congregation here prefent ; that with meek heart and due reverence they may hear and receive thy holy word, truly ferving thee in holinefs and righteoufnefs all the days of their life. And we moft humbly befeech thee of thy goodnefs, O Lord, to comfort and fuccour all them, who in this tranfitory life are in trouble, forrow, need, ficknefs, or any other adverfity. And we alfo blefs thy holy Name, for all thy fervants departed this life in thy faith and fear ; befeeching thee to give us grace fo to follow their good examples, that with them we may be partakers of thy heavenly kingdom. Grant this, O Father, for Jefus Chrift's fake, our only Mediator and Advocate. *Amen.*

*Then fhall the Elder fay to them that come to receive the Holy Communion.*

YE that do truly and earneftly repent of your fins, and are in love and charity with your neighbours, and intend to lead a new life, following the commandments of God, and walking from henceforth in his holy ways ; Draw near with faith, and take this holy Sacrament to your comfort ; and make your humble confeffion to Almighty God, meekly kneeling upon your knees.

*Then*

*Then shall this general Confession be made by the Mi-
nister in the Name of all those that are minded to
receive the Holy Communion, both he and all the
people kneeling humbly upon their knees, and saying,*

ALmighty God, Father of our Lord Jesus Christ,
Maker of all things, Judge of all men ; We
acknowledge and bewail our manifold sins and
wickedness, Which we from time to time most
grievously have committed, By thought, word, and
deed, against thy Divine Majesty, provoking most
justly thy wrath and indignation against us. We
do earnestly repent, and are heartily sorry for these
our misdoings ; The remembrance of them is
grievous unto us. Have mercy upon us, have
mercy upon us, most merciful Father ; For thy
Son our Lord Jesus Christ's sake, forgive us all that
is past ; And grant, that we may ever hereafter
serve and please thee in newness of life, To the
honour and glory of thy Name, Through Jesus
Christ our Lord. *Amen.*

*Then shall the Elder say,*

O Almighty God, our heavenly Father, who of
thy great mercy hast promised forgiveness of
sins to all them that with hearty repentance and
true faith turn unto thee ; Have mercy upon us ;
pardon and deliver us from all our sins, confirm
and strengthen us in all goodness, and bring us to
everlasting life, through Jesus Christ our Lord.
*Amen.*

*Then all standing, the Elder shall say.*

Hear what comfortable words our Saviour Christ
saith unto all that truly turn to him :
COME unto me, all ye that are burdened and
heavy-laden, and I will refresh you. *Matth.*
**xi. 28,**

So

So God loved the world, that he gave his only-begotten Son, to the end that all that believe in him, fhould not perifh, but have everlafting life. *John* iii. 16.

Hear alfo what St. Paul faith :

This is a true faying, and worthy of all men to be received, That Chrift Jefus came into the world to fave finners. 1 *Tim.* i. 15.

Hear alfo what St. John faith :

If any man fin, we have an Advocate with the Father, Jefus Chrift the righteous : and he is the propitiation for our fins. 1 *John*, ii. 1, 2.

*After which the Elder fhall proceed, faying,*

Lift up your hearts.
*Anfw.* We lift them up unto the Lord.
*Elder.* Let us give thanks unto our Lord God.
*Anfw.* It is meet and right fo to do.

*Then fhall the Elder fay,*

IT is very meet, right, and our bounden duty, that we fhould at all times, and in all places, give thanks unto thee, O Lord, Holy Father †, Almighty, Everlafting God.

*Here fhall follow the proper Preface, according to the Time, if there be any efpecially appointed; or elfe immediately fhall follow ;*

THerefore with Angels and Archangels and with all the company of heaven, we laud and magnify thy glorious Name, evermore praifing thee, and faying, Holy, holy, holy, Lord God of hofts, heaven and earth are full of thy glory. Glory be to thee, O Lord moft high. Amen.

---

† *Thefe Words* [Holy Father] *muft be omitted on Trinity Sunday.*

*Proper Prefaces.*

### Upon *Chriſtmas-day.*

BEcauſe thou didſt give Jeſus Chriſt thine only Son to be born as at this time for us, who, by the operation of the Holy Ghoſt, was made very man, and that without ſpot of ſin, to make us clean from all ſin. Therefore with Angels, *&c.*

### Upon *Eaſter-day.*

BUT chiefly we are bound to praiſe thee for the glorious Reſurrection of thy Son Jeſus Chriſt our Lord : for he is the very Paſchal Lamb, which was offered for us, and hath taken away the ſin of the world ; who by his death hath deſtroyed death, and by his riſing to life again, hath reſtored to us everlaſting life. Therefore with Angels, *&c.*

### Upon *Aſcenſion-day.*

THrough thy moſt dearly beloved Son, Jeſus Chriſt our Lord ; who, after his moſt glorious Reſurrection, manifeſtly appeared to all his Apoſtles, and in their ſight aſcended up into heaven, to prepare a place for us ; that where he is, thither we might alſo aſcend, and reign with him in glory. Therefore with angels, *&c.*

### Upon *Whitſunday.*

THrough Jeſus Chriſt our Lord ; according to whoſe moſt true promiſe the Holy Ghoſt came down, as at this time, from heaven with a ſudden great ſound, as it had been a mighty wind, in the likeneſs of fiery tongues, lighting upon the Apoſtles, to teach them, and to lead them to all truth ; giving them both the gift of divers languages, and alſo boldneſs, with fervent zeal, conſtantly to preach the Goſpel unto all nations, whereby we have been
brought

brought out of darknefs and error, into the clear light and true knowledge of thee, and of thy Son Jefus Chrift. Therefore with Angels, &c.

*Upon the Feaft of Trinity.*

WHO art one God, one Lord; not one only perfon, but three perfons in one fubftance. For that which we believe of the glory of the Father, the fame we believe of the Son, and of the Holy Ghoft, without any difference or inequality. Therefore with Angels, &c.

*After each of which Prefaces fhall immediately be faid,*

THerefore with Angels and Archangels, and with all the company of heaven, we laud and magnify thy glorious Name, evermore praifing thee, and faying, Holy, holy, holy, Lord God of hofts, heaven and earth are full of thy glory. Glory be to thee, O Lord moft high. *Amen.*

*Then fhall the Elder, kneeling down at the Table, fay, in the Name of all them that fhall receive the Communion, this Prayer following; the People alfo kneeling.*

WE do not prefume to come to this thy Table, O merciful Lord, trufting in our own righteoufnefs, but in thy manifold and great mercies. We are not worthy fo much as to gather up the crumbs under thy table. But thou art the fame Lord, whofe property is always to have mercy: Grant us therefore, gracious Lord, fo to eat the flefh of thy dear Son Jefus Chrift, and to drink his blood, that our finful bodies may be made clean by his body, and our fouls wafhed through his moft precious blood, and that we may evermore dwell in him, and he in us. *Amen.*

*Then the Elder fhall fay the Prayer of Confecration, as followeth:*

ALmighty God, our heavenly Father, who, of thy tender mercy, didft give thine only Son Jefus Chrift to fuffer death upon the crofs for our

F 8 redemption;

redemption; who made there (by his oblation of himself once offered) a full, perfect, and sufficient sacrifice, oblation, and satisfaction for the sins of the whole world; and did institute, and in his holy Gospel command us to continue, a perpetual memory of that his precious death until his coming again; hear us, O merciful Father, we most humbly beseech thee, and grant that we, receiving these thy creatures of bread and wine, according to thy Son our Saviour Jesus Christ's holy institution, in remembrance of his death and passion, may be partakers of his most blessed Body and Blood: who, in the same night that he was betrayed \* took bread; and when he had given thanks, he brake it †; and gave it to his disciples, saying, Take, eat; ‡ this is my Body which is given for you; do this in remembrance of me. Likewise after Supper § he took the Cup; and when he had given thanks, he gave it to them, saying, Drink ye all of this; for this ‖ is my Blood of the New Testament, which is shed for you, and for many, for the remission of sins: Do this as oft as ye shall drink it, in remembrance of me. *Amen.*

\* *Here the Elder is to take the Patten into his Hands:*

† *And here to break the Bread:*

‡ *And here to lay his Hand upon all the Bread.*

§ *Here he is to take the Cup into his Hand:*

‖ *And here to lay his Hand upon every Vessel (be it Chalice or Flaggon) in which there is any Wine to be consecrated.*

*Then shall the Minister first receive the Communion in both kinds himself, and then proceed to deliver the same to the other Ministers in like manner, (if any be present) and after that to the People also, in order, into their Hands. And when he delivereth the Bread to any one, he shall say,*

THE Body of our Lord Jesus Christ, which was given for thee, preserve thy body and soul unto everlasting life. Take and eat this in remembrance

brance that Chrift died for thee, and feed on him in thy heart by faith with thankfgiving.

*And the Minifter that delivereth the Cup to any one fhall fay,*

THE Blood of our Lord Jefus Chrift, which was fhed for thee, preferve thy body and foul unto everlafting life. Drink this in remembrance that Chrift's Blood was fhed for thee, and be thankful.

*If the confecrated Bread or Wine be all fpent before all have communicated, the Elder may confecrate more, by repeating the Prayer of Confecration.*

*When all have communicated, the Minifter fhall return to the Lord's Table, and place upon it what remaineth of the confecrated Elements, couering the fame with a fair Linen Cloth.*

*Then fhall the Elder fay the Lord's Prayer, the People repeating after him every Petition.*

OUR Father who art in Heaven, Hallowed be thy Name; Thy kingdom come; Thy Will be done on Earth, As it is in Heaven : Give us this day our daily bread ; And forgive us our trefpaffes, As we forgive them that trefpafs againft us ; And lead us not into temptation ; But deliver us from evil : For thine is the Kingdom, and the Power, and the Glory, For ever and ever. *Amen.*

*After which fhall be faid as followeth :*

O Lord and heavenly Father, we thy humble fervants defire thy Fatherly goodnefs mercifully to accept this our facrifice of praife and thankfgiving; moft humbly befeeching thee to grant that, by the merits and death of thy Son Jefus Chrift, and through faith in his blood, we and all thy whole Church may obtain remiffion of our fins, and all other benefits of his paffion. And here we offer
and

and prefent unto thee, O Lord, ourfelves, our fouls and bodies, to be a reafonable, holy, and lively facrifice unto thee ; humbly befeeching thee that all we who are partakers of this holy Communion, may be filled with thy grace and heavenly benediction. And although we be unworthy, through our manifold fins, to offer unto thee any facrifice, yet we befeech thee to accept this our bounden duty and fervice; not weighing our merits, but pardoning our offences, through Jefus Chrift our Lord ; by whom, and with whom, in the unity of the Holy Ghoft, all honour and glory be unto thee, O Father Almighty, world without end. *Amen.*

### *Then fhall be faid,*

GLory be to God on high, and on earth peace, good-will towards men. We praife thee, we blefs thee, we worfhip thee, we glorify thee, we give thanks to thee for thy great glory, O Lord God, heavenly king, God the Father Almighty.

O Lord, the only-begotten Son Jefu Chrift; O Lord God, Lamb of God, Son of the Father, that takeft away the fins of the world, have mercy upon us. Thou that takeft away the fins of the world, have mercy upon us. Thou that takeft away the fins of the world, receive our prayer. Thou that fitteft at the right hand of God the Father, have mercy upon us.

For thou only art holy, thou only art the Lord, thou only, O Chrift, with the Holy Ghoft, art moft high in the glory of God the Father. *Amen.*

*Then the Elder, if he fee it expedient, may put up an Extempore Prayer ; and afterwards fhall let the People depart with this Bleffing :*

MAY the peace of God, which paffeth all underftanding, keep your hearts and minds in the knowledge and love of God, and of his Son
Jefus

Jefus Chrift our Lord; and the bleffing of God Almighty, the Father, the Son, and the Holy Ghoft, be amongft you, and remain with you always. *Amen.*

---

## The MINISTRATION of BAPTISM of INFANTS.

*The Minifter coming to the Font, which is to be filled with pure Water, fhall fay,*

DEarly beloved, forafmuch as all men are con-ceived and born in fin, and that our Saviour Chrift faith, None can enter into the kingdom of God, except he be regenerate and born anew of water and of the Holy Ghoft; I befeech you to call upon God the Father, through our Lord Jefus Chrift, that of his bounteous mercy he will grant to *this Child* that thing which by nature *he* cannot have; that *he* may be baptized with water and the Holy Ghoft, and received into Chrift's holy Church, and be made a *lively member* of the fame.

*Then fhall the Minifter fay,*

Let us pray.

ALmighty and everlafting God, who of thy great mercy didft fave Noah and his family in the ark from perifhing by water; and alfo didft fafely lead the children of Ifrael, thy people, through the Red Sea, figuring thereby thy holy Baptifm; and by the Baptifm of thy well-beloved Son Jefus Chrift in the river Jordan, didft fanctify water to the myftical wafhing away of fin, We befeech thee, for thine infinite mercies, that thou wilt look upon *this Child*; wafh *him* and fanctify *him* with the Holy Ghoft; that *he* being delivered from thy wrath,

wrath, may be received into the ark of Chriſt's Church; and being ſtedfaſt in faith, joyful through hope, and rooted in charity, may ſo paſs the waves of this troubleſome world, that finally *he* may come to the land of everlaſting life; there to reign with thee, world without end, through Jeſus Chriſt our Lord. *Amen.*

A Lmighty and immortal God, the aid of all that need, the helper of all that flee to thee for ſuccour, the life of them that believe, and the reſurrection of the dead, we call upon thee for *this Infant*, that *he*, coming to thy holy Baptiſm, may receive remiſſion of *his* ſins by ſpiritual regeneration. Receive *him*, O Lord, as thou haſt promiſed by thy well-beloved Son, ſaying, Aſk, and ye ſhall have; ſeek, and ye ſhall find; knock, and it ſhall be opened unto you: So give now unto us that aſk; let us that ſeek find; open the gate unto us that knock; that *this Infant* may enjoy the everlaſting benediction of thy heavenly waſhing, and may come to the eternal kingdom which thou haſt promiſed by Chriſt our Lord. *Amen.*

*Then ſhall the People ſtand up; and the Miniſter ſhall ſay,*

Hear the words of the Goſpel written by Saint *Mark*, in the Tenth Chapter, at the Thirteenth Verſe.

T HEY brought young children to Chriſt, that he ſhould touch them. And his diſciples rebuked thoſe that brought them; but when Jeſus ſaw it he was much diſpleaſed, and ſaid unto them, Suffer the little children to come unto me, and forbid them not, for of ſuch is the kingdom of God. Verily, I ſay unto you, Whoſoever ſhall not receive the kingdom of God as a little child, he ſhall

not

not enter therein. And he took them up in his arms, put his hands upon them, and bleſſed them.

*Then ſhall the Miniſter ſay,*

ALmighty and everlaſting God, heavenly Father, we give thee humble thanks, that thou haſt vouchſafed to call us to the knowledge of thy grace, and faith in thee : Increaſe this knowledge, and confirm this faith in us evermore. Give thy Holy Spirit to *this Infant,* that *he* may be born again, and be made *an heir* of everlaſting ſalvation, through our Lord Jeſus Chriſt, who liveth and reigneth with thee and the Holy Spirit, now and for ever. *Amen.*

O Merciful God, grant that the old Adam in *this Child* may be ſo buried, that the new man may be raiſed up in *him.* *Amen.*

Grant that all carnal affections may die in *him,* and that all things belonging to the Spirit may live and grow in *him.* *Amen.*

Grant that *he* may have power and ſtrength to have victory, and to triumph againſt the devil, the world, and the fleſh. *Amen.*

Grant that whoſoever is dedicated to thee by our office and miniſtry, may alſo be endued with heavenly virtues, and everlaſtingly rewarded, through thy mercy, O bleſſed Lord God, who doſt live and govern all things, world without end. *Amen.*

ALmighty everliving God, whoſe moſt dearly beloved Son Jeſus Chriſt, for the forgiveneſs of our ſins, did ſhed out of his moſt precious ſide both water and blood ; and gave commandment to his diſciples, that they ſhould go teach all nations, and baptize them, in the Name of the Father, and of the Son, and of the Holy Ghoſt : Regard, we beſeech thee, the ſupplications of thy congregation ; ſanctify this water to the myſtical waſhing away of

F 11                                        ſin ;

fin ; and grant that *this Child,* now to be baptized, may receive the fulnefs of thy grace, and ever remain in the number of thy faithful and elect children, through Jefus Chrift our Lord. *Amen.*

*Then the Minifter fhall take the Child into his Hands, and fay to the Friends of the Child,*

Name this Child.

*And then, naming it after them, he fhall dip it in the Water, or fprinkle it therewith, faying,*

N. I baptize thee, In the Name of the Father, and of the Son, and of the Holy Ghoft. *Amen.*

*Then the Minifter fhall fay,*

WE receive this Child into the Congregation of Chrift's flock, and * fign *him* with the fign of the Crofs ; in token that hereafter *he* fhall not be afhamed to confefs the faith of Chrift crucified, and manfully to fight under his banner againft fin, the world and the devil ; and to continue Chrift's faithful foldier and fervant unto his life's end. *Amen.*

*\* Here the Minifter fhall make a Crofs upon the Child's Forehead.*

*Then fhall the Minifter fay,*

SEeing now, dearly beloved brethren, that *this Child is* grafted into the body of Chrift's Church, let us give thanks unto Almighty God for thefe benefits, and with one accord make our prayers unto him, that *this Child* may lead the reft of *his life* according to this beginning.

*Then fhall be faid, all kneeling,*

OUR Father, who art in heaven, Hallowed be thy Name ; Thy kingdom come ; Thy will be done on earth, as it is in heaven : Give us this day cur daily bread ; and forgive us our trefpaffes, paſſes, as we forgive them that treſpaſs againſt us; And lead us not into temptation; But deliver us from evil. *Amen.*

WE yield thee hearty thanks, moſt merciful Father, that it hath pleaſed thee to receive *this Infant* for thine own *Child* by adoption, and to incorporate *him* into thy holy Church. And humbly we beſeech thee to grant, that *he,* being dead unto ſin, and living unto righteouſneſs, and being buried with Chriſt in his death, may crucify the old man, and utterly aboliſh the whole body of ſin; and that, as *he is* made *partaker* of the death of thy Son, *he* may alſo be *partaker* of his reſurrection; ſo that finally, with the reſidue of thy holy Church, *he* may be *an inheritor* of thine everlaſting kingdom, through Chriſt our Lord. *Amen.*

---

## The Miniſtration of Baptism to ſuch as are of Riper Years.

*The Miniſter ſhall ſay,*

DEarly beloved, foraſmuch as all men are conceived and born in ſin (and that which is born of the fleſh is fleſh, and they that are in the fleſh cannot pleaſe God, but live in ſin, committing many actual tranſgreſſions); and that our Saviour Chriſt ſaith, None can enter into the kingdom of God, except he be regenerate and born anew of water and of the Holy Ghoſt; I beſeech you to call upon God the Father, through our Lord Jeſus Chriſt, that of his bounteous goodneſs he will grant to *theſe Perſons,* that which by nature *they* cannot have; that *they* may be baptized with Water and the Holy Ghoſt, and received into Chriſt's holy Church, and be made lively *members* of the ſame.

*Then*

*Then fhall the Minifter fay,*

Let us pray.

*(And here all the Congregation fhall kneel.)*

ALmighty and everlafting God, who of thy great mercy didft fave Noah and his family in the ark from perifhing by water ; and alfo didft fafely lead the children of Ifrael thy people through the Red Sea, figuring thereby thy holy Baptifm ; and by the Baptifm of thy well-beloved Son Jefus Chrift in the river Jordan, didft fanctify the element of water to the myftical wafhing away of fin ; We befeech thee, for thine infinite mercies, that thou wilt mercifully look upon *thefe* thy *Servants* ; wafh *them* and fanctify *them* with the Holy Ghoft ; that *they* being delivered from thy wrath, may be received into the ark of Chrift's Church ; and being ftedfaft in faith, joyful through hope, and rooted in charity, may fo pafs the waves of this troublefome world, that finally *they* may come to the land of everlafting life ; there to reign with thee, world without end, through Jefus Chrift our Lord. *Amen.*

ALmighty and immortal God, the aid of all that need, the helper of all that flee to thee for fuccour, the life of them that believe, and the refurrection of the dead ; We call upon thee for *thefe Perfons* ; that *they*, coming to thy holy Baptifm, may receive remiffion of *their* fins by fpiritual regeneration. Receive *them*, O Lord, as thou haft promifed by thy well beloved Son, faying, Afk, and ye fhall receive ; feek, and ye fhall find ; knock, and it fhall be opened unto you : So give now unto us that afk ; let us that feek find ; open the gate unto us that knock ; that *thefe Perfons* may enjoy the everlafting benediction of thy heavenly wafhing, and may come to the eternal kingdom which thou haft promifed by Chrift our Lord. *Amen.*

2

*Then*

*Then fhall the People ftand up, and the Minifter fhall fay,*

Hear the words of the Gofpel written by Saint *John,* in the third Chapter, beginning at the firft Verfe.

THERE was a man of the Pharifees, named Nicodemus, a ruler of the Jews: The fame came to Jefus by night, and faid unto him, Rabbi, we know that thou art a teacher come from God; for no man can do thefe miracles that thou doeft, except God be with him. Jefus anfwered and faid unto him, Verily, verily, I fay unto thee, Except a man be born again, he cannot fee the kingdom of God. Nicodemus faith unto him, How can a man be born when he is old? Can he enter the fecond time into his mother's womb, and be born? Jefus anfwered, Verily, verily, I fay unto thee, Except a man be born of water, and of the Spirit, he cannot enter into the kingdom of God. That which is born of the flefh, is flefh; and that which is born of the Spirit, is fpirit. Marvel not that I faid unto thee, Ye muft be born again. The wind bloweth where it lifteth, and thou heareft the found thereof; but canft not tell whence it cometh, and whither it goeth: fo is every one that is born of the Spirit.

*After which he fhall fay,*

ALmighty and everlafting God, heavenly Father, we give thee humble thanks, for that thou haft vouchfafed to call us to the knowledge of thy grace, and faith in thee: Increafe this knowledge, and confirm this faith in us evermore. Give thy Holy Spirit to *thefe Perfons,* that *they* may be born again, and be made *heirs* of everlafting falvation, through our Lord Jefus

G                                                   Chrift,

Chrift, who liveth and reigneth with thee and the Holy Spirit, now and for ever. *Amen.*

*Then the Minister shall speak to the* Perfons *to be baptized, on this wife:*

WELL beloved, who *are* come hither, defiring to receive holy Baptifm, *ye* have heard how the Congregation hath prayed, that our Lord Jefus Chrift would vouchfafe to receive you, and blefs you, to releafe you of your fins, to give you the kingdom of heaven, and everlafting life. And our Lord Jefus Chrift hath promifed in his holy word, to grant all thofe things that we have prayed for; which promife he for his part will moft furely keep and perform.

Wherefore, after this promife made by Chrift, *you* muft alfo faithfully for *your* part promife, in the prefence of this whole Congregation, that *you* will renounce the devil and all his works, and conftantly believe God's holy Word, and obediently keep his Commandments.

*Then shall the Minister demand of each of the Perfons to be baptized, feverally,*

*Quest.* DOST thou renounce the devil and all his works, the vain pomp and glory of the world, with all covetous defires of the fame, and the carnal defires of the flefh, fo that thou wilt not follow, or be led by them?

*Answ.* I renounce them all.

*Quest.* DOST thou believe in God the Father Almighty, Maker of heaven and earth.

And in Jefus Chrift his only begotten Son our Lord? And that he was conceived by the Holy Ghoft; born of the Virgin Mary; that he fuffered under Pontius Pilate, was crucified, dead, and buried;

buried ; that he went down into hell, and alfo did rife again the third day ; that he afcended into heaven, and fitteth at the right hand of God the Father Almighty ; and from thence fhall come again, at the end of the world, to judge the quick and the dead ?

And doft thou believe in the Holy Ghoft ; the Holy Catholic Church ; the Communion of Saints ; the Remiffion of Sins ; the Refurrection of the Body ; and everlafting Life after Death ?

*Anfw.* All this I ftedfaftly believe.

*Queft.* WILT thou be baptized in this faith ?
   *Anfw.* This is my defire.

*Queft.* WILT thou then obediently keep God's holy will and commandments, and walk in the fame all the days of thy life ?

*Anfw.* I will endeavour fo to do, God being my helper.

*Then fhall the Minifter fay,*

O Merciful God, grant that the old Adam in *thefe Perfons* may be fo buried, that the new man may be raifed up in *them. Amen.*

Grant that all carnal affections may die in *them,* and that all things belonging to the Spirit may live and grow in *them. Amen.*

Grant that *they* may have power and ftrength to have victory, and to triumph againft the devil, the world, and the flefh. *Amen.*

Grant that *they* being here dedicated to thee by our Office and Miniftry, may alfo be endued with heavenly virtues, and everlaftingly rewarded, through thy mercy, O bleffed Lord God, who doft live and govern all things, world without end. *Amen.*

      Almighty

ALmighty everliving God, whoſe moſt dearly beloved Son Jeſus Chriſt, for the forgiveneſs of our ſins, did ſhed out of his moſt precious ſide both water and blood ; and gave commandment to his diſciples, that they ſhould go teach all nations, and baptize them, in the Name of the Father, and of the Son, and of the Holy Ghoſt : Regard, we beſeech thee, the ſupplications of this congregation ; ſanctify this water to the myſtical waſhing away of ſin ; and grant that the *Perſons* now to be baptized, may receive the fulneſs of thy grace, and ever remain in the number of thy faithful and elect children, through Jeſus Chriſt our Lord. *Amen.*

*Then ſhall the Miniſter take each Perſon to be baptized by the Right Hand; and placing him conveniently by the Font, according to his Diſcretion, ſhall aſk the Name ; and then ſhall dip him in the Water, or pour Water upon him, ſaying,*

N. I baptize thee, In the Name of the Father, and of the Son, and of the Holy Ghoſt. *Amen.*

*Then ſhall the Miniſter ſay,*

SEeing now, dearly beloved brethren, that *theſe Perſons are* grafted into the body of Chriſt's Church ; let us give thanks unto Almighty God for theſe benefits, and with one accord make our prayers unto him, that *they* may lead the reſt of *their* life according to this beginning.

*Then ſhall be ſaid the Lord's Prayer, all kneeling.*

OUR Father, who art in heaven, Hallowed be thy Name ; Thy kingdom come ; Thy will be done on earth, as it is in heaven : Give us this day our daily bread ; and forgive us our treſpaſſes, as we forgive them that treſpaſs againſt us ;

And

And lead us not into temptation ; But deliver us from evil. *Amen.*

WE yield thee humble thanks, O heavenly Father, that thou haſt vouchſafed to call us to the knowledge of thy grace, and faith in thee ; Increaſe this knowledge, and confirm this faith in us evermore. Give thy Holy Spirit to *theſe Perſons*; that being born again, and made *heirs* of everlaſting ſalvation, through our Lord Jeſus Chriſt, *they* may continue thy *ſervants*, and attain thy promiſes, through the ſame Lord Jeſus Chriſt thy Son; who liveth and reigneth with thee, in the unity of the ſame Holy Spirit, everlaſtingly. *Amen.*

---

## The Form of Solemnization of MATRIMONY.

*Firſt, the Banns of all that are to be married together, muſt be publiſhed in the Congregation, three ſeveral Sundays, in the Time of Divine Service ; the Miniſter ſaying after the accuſtomed Manner,*

I Publiſh the Banns of Marriage between *M.* of —— and *N.* of ——. If any of you know cauſe or juſt impediment, why theſe two perſons ſhould not be joined together in holy Matrimony, ye are to declare it : This is the firſt [*ſecond*, or *third*] time of aſking.

*At the Day and Time appointed for Solemnization of Matrimony, the Perſons to be married, ſtanding together, the Man on the Right Hand, and the Woman on the Left, the Miniſter ſhall ſay,*

DEarly beloved, we are gathered together here in the ſight of God, and in the face of this Congregation, to join together this Man and this

Woman

Woman in holy Matrimony; which is an honourable eſtate, inſtituted of God in the time of man's innocency, ſignifying unto us the myſtical union that is betwixt Chriſt and his Church: which holy eſtate Chriſt adorned and beautified with his preſence, and firſt miracle that he wrought in *Cana* of *Galilee,* and is commended of St. *Paul* to be honourable among all men; and therefore is not by any to be enterprized, or taken in hand unadviſedly, lightly or wantonly, to ſatisfy men's carnal luſts and appetites, like brute beaſts, that have no underſtanding; but reverently, diſcreetly, adviſedly, ſoberly, and in the fear of God; duly conſidering the cauſes for which Matrimony was ordained.

Firſt, It was ordained for the procreation of children, to be brought up in the fear and nurture of the Lord, and to the praiſe of his holy Name.

Secondly, It was ordained for a remedy againſt ſin, and to avoid fornication; that ſuch perſons as have not the gift of continency, might marry, and keep themſelves undefiled members of Chriſt's body.

Thirdly, It was ordained for the mutual ſociety, help, and comfort, that the one ought to have of the other, both in proſperity and adverſity.

Into which holy eſtate theſe two perſons preſent come now to be joined. Therefore if any man can ſhew any juſt cauſe why they may not lawfully be joined together, let him now ſpeak, or elſe hereafter for ever hold his peace.

*And alſo ſpeaking unto the Perſons that are to be married, he ſhall ſay,*

I Require and charge you both (as you will anſwer at the dreadful day of judgment, when the ſecrets of all hearts ſhall be diſcloſed) that if either of you know any impediment why you may not be lawfully

lawfully joined together in Matrimony, you do now confefs it. For be ye well affured, that fo many as are coupled together otherwife than God's Word doth allow, are not joined together by God, neither is their Matrimony lawful.

*If no Impediment be alledged, then fhall the Minifter fay unto the Man,*

*M.* WILT thou have this woman to thy wedded wife, to live together after God's ordinance, in the holy eftate of Matrimony? Wilt thou love her, comfort her, honour, and keep her, in ficknefs, and in health; and forfaking all other, keep thee only unto her, fo long as you both fhall live?

*The Man fhall anfwer,*
I will.

*Then fhall the Minifter fay unto the Woman,*

*N.* WILT thou have this Man to thy wedded Hufband, to live together after God's ordinance, in the holy eftate of Matrimony? Wilt thou obey him, ferve him, love, honour, and keep him, in ficknefs and in health; and forfaking all other, keep thee only unto him, fo long as you both fhall live?

*The Woman fhall anfwer,*
I will.

*Then the Minifter fhall caufe the Man with his Right Hand to take the woman by her Right Hand, and to fay after him as followeth:*

I *M.* take thee *N.* to be my wedded wife, to have and to hold, from this day forward, for better for worfe, for richer for poorer, in ficknefs, and in health, to love and to cherifh, till death us do part, according to God's holy ordinance; and thereto I plight thee my Faith.

G 4                    *Then*

*Then shall they loose their Hands, and the Woman with her Right Hand taking the Man by his Right Hand, shall likewise say after the Minister :*

I N. take thee *M.* to be my wedded Husband, to have and to hold, from this day forward, for better for worse, for richer for poorer, in sickness and in health, to love, cherish, and to obey, till death us do part, according to God's holy ordinance ; and thereto I give thee my Faith.

*Then the Minister shall say,*

Let us pray.

O Eternal God, Creator and Preserver of all mankind, Giver of all spiritual grace, the Author of everlasting life; Send thy blessing upon these thy servants, this Man and this Woman, whom we bless in thy Name ; that as Isaac and Rebecca lived faithfully together, so these persons may surely perform and keep the vow and covenant betwixt them made, and may ever remain in perfect love and peace together, and live according to thy laws, through Jesus Christ our Lord. *Amen.*

*Then shall the Minister join their Right Hands together, and say,*

Those whom God hath joined together, let no man put asunder.

*Then shall the Minister speak unto the People :*

FOrasmuch as *M.* and *N.* have consented together in holy wedlock, and have witnessed the same before God and this company, and thereto have pledged their faith either to other, and have declared the same by joining of hands; I pronounce that they are Man and Wife together, In the Name of the Father, and of the Son, and of the Holy Ghost. *Amen.*

*And*

*And the Minifter fhall add this bleffing :*

GOD the Father, God the Son, God the Holy Ghoſt, bleſs, preſerve, and keep you; the Lord mercifully with his favour look upon you, and ſo fill you with all ſpiritual benediction and grace, that ye may ſo live together in this life, that in the world to come ye may have life everlaſting. *Amen.*

*Then the Minifter fhall fay,*

Lord, have mercy upon us.
*Anfw.* Chriſt, have mercy upon us.
*Minifter.* Lord, have mercy upon us.

OUR Father, who art in heaven, Hallowed be thy Name; thy kingdom come; Thy will be done on earth, as it is in heaven : Give us this day our daily bread; And forgive us our trefpaffes, as we forgive them that trefpaſs againſt us : And lead us not into temptation ; but deliver us from evil. *Amen.*

*Minifter.* O Lord, ſave thy ſervant and thy handmaid.
*Anfwer.* And let them put their truſt in thee.
*Minifter.* O Lord, ſend them help from thy holy place;
*Anfwer.* And evermore defend them.
*Minifter.* Be unto them a tower of ſtrength,
*Anfwer.* From the face of their enemy.
*Minifter* O Lord, hear our prayer;
*Anfwer.* And let our cry come unto thee.

*Minifter.*

O God of Abraham, God of Iſaac, God of Jacob, bleſs theſe thy ſervants, and ſow the ſeed of eternal life in their hearts, that whatſoever in thy holy Word they ſhall profitably learn, they may in deed fulfil the ſame. Look, O Lord, mercifully upon them from heaven, and bleſs them.

And

And as thou didſt ſend thy bleſſing upon Abraham and Sarah, to their great comfort ; ſo vouchſafe to ſend thy bleſſing upon theſe thy ſervants ; that they obeying thy will, and always being in ſafety under thy protection, may abide in thy love unto their lives end, through Jeſus Chriſt our Lord. *Amen.*

*This Prayer next following ſhall be omitted, where the Woman is paſt child-bearing.*

O Merciful Lord and heavenly Father, by whoſe gracious gift mankind is increaſed ; We beſeech thee, aſſiſt with thy bleſſing theſe two perſons, that they may both be fruitful in the procreation of children, and alſo live together ſo long in godly love and honeſty, that they may ſee their children chriſtianly and virtuouſly brought up, to thy praiſe and honour, through Jeſus Chriſt our Lord. *Amen.*

O God, who by thy mighty power haſt made all things of nothing, who alſo (after other things ſet in order) didſt appoint that out of man (created after thine own image and ſimilitude) woman ſhould take her beginning : and knitting them together, didſt teach that it ſhould never be lawful to put aſunder thoſe whom thou by Matrimony hadſt made one ; O God, who haſt conſecrated the ſtate of Matrimony to ſuch an excellent myſtery, that in it is ſignified and repreſented the ſpiritual marriage and unity betwixt Chriſt and his Church ; Look mercifully upon theſe thy ſervants, that both this man may love his wife, according to thy Word (as Chriſt did love his ſpouſe the Church, who gave himſelf for it, loving and cheriſhing it, even as his own fleſh), and alſo that this woman may be loving and amiable, faithful and obedient to her huſband : and in all quietneſs, ſobriety, and peace, be a follower of holy and godly matrons. O Lord, bleſs them both, and grant them

to

to inherit thy everlasting kingdom, through Jesus Christ our Lord. *Amen.*

*Then shall the Minister say,*

ALmighty God, who at the beginning did create our first parents, Adam and Eve, and did sanctify and join them together in marriage; Pour upon you the riches of his grace, sanctify and bless you, that ye may please him both in body and soul, and live together in holy love unto your lives end. *Amen.*

## The COMMUNION of the SICK.

*The Collect.*

ALmighty, everliving God, maker of mankind, who dost correct those whom thou dost love, and chastise every one whom thou dost receive; we beseech thee to have mercy upon this thy servant visited with thine hand; and to grant that *he* may take *his* sickness patiently, and recover *his* bodily health, if it be thy gracious will; and whensoever *his* soul shall depart from the body, it may be without spot presented unto thee, through Jesus Christ our Lord. *Amen.*

*The Epistle.* Heb. xii. 5, 6.

MY son, despise not thou the chastening of the Lord, nor faint when thou art rebuked of him : for whom the Lord loveth he chasteneth, and scourgeth every son whom he receiveth.

*The Gospel.* John, v. 24.

VErily, verily, I say unto you, He that heareth my word, and believeth on him that sent me, hath everlasting life, and shall not come into condemnation; but is passed from death unto life.

G 6

*After*

*After which the Elder shall proceed according to the form before prescribed for the Holy Communion, beginning at these words [Ye that do truly, &c.]*

*At the time of the distribution of the Holy Sacrament, the Elder shall first receive the Communion himself, and after minister unto them that are appointed to communicate with the sick, and last of all to the sick person.*

---

## The Order for the BURIAL of the DEAD.

*The Minister meeting the Corpse, and going before it, shall say,*

I Am the resurrection and the life, saith the Lord: he that believeth in me, though he were dead, yet shall he live : and whosoever liveth and believeth in me, shall never die. *John,* xi. 25, 26.

I Know that my Redeemer liveth, and that he shall stand at the latter day upon the earth. And though after my skin, worms destroy this body, yet in my flesh shall I see God : whom I shall see for myself, and mine eyes shall behold, and not another. *Job.* xix. 25, 26, 27.

WE brought nothing into this world, and it is certain we can carry nothing out. The Lord gave, and the Lord hath taken away; blessed be the Name of the Lord. I *Tim.* vi. 7. *Job,* i. 21.

*Then shall be read,* Psal. xc.

L ORD, thou hast been our refuge from one generation to another.

Before the mountains were brought forth, or ever the earth and the world were made, thou art God from everlasting, and world without end.

Thou turnest man to destruction : again thou sayest, Come again, ye children of men.

For

For a thoufand years in thy fight are but as yefterday; feeing that is paft, as a watch in the night.

As foon as thou fcattereft them, they are even as a fleep, and fade away fuddenly like the grafs.

In the morning it is green, and groweth up: but in the evening it is cut down, dried up, and withered.

For we confume away in thy difpleafure; and are afraid at thy wrathful indignation.

Thou haft fet our mifdeeds before thee, and our fecret fins in the light of thy countenance.

For when thou art angry, all our days are gone: we bring our years to an end, as it were a tale that is told.

The days of our age are threefcore years and ten; and though men be fo ftrong, that they come to fourfcore years, yet is their ftrength then but labour and forrow: fo foon paffeth it away, and we are gone.

But who regardeth the power of thy wrath: for even according to thy fear, fo is thy difpleafure.

So teach us to number our days, that we may apply our hearts unto wifdom.

Turn thee again, O Lord, at the laft, and be gracious unto thy fervants.

O fatisfy us with thy mercy, and that foon; fo fhall we rejoice and be glad all the days of our life.

Comfort us again now after the time that thou haft plagued us, and for the years wherein we have fuffered adverfity.

Shew thy fervants thy work, and their children thy glory.

And the glorious majefty of the Lord our God be upon us: profper thou the work of our hands upon us, O profper thou our handy-work.

Glory be to the Father, and to the Son, and to the Holy Ghoft;

**As**

As it was in the beginning, is now, and ever ſhall be, world without end. *Amen.*

*Then ſhall follow the Leſſon taken out of the fifteenth chapter of the firſt Epiſtle of Saint Paul to the Corinthians.*

### 1 Cor. xv. 20.

NOW is Chriſt riſen from the dead, and become the firſt-fruits of them that ſlept For ſince by man came death, by man came alſo the reſurrection of the dead. For as in Adam all die, even ſo in Chriſt ſhall all be made alive. But every man in his own order; Chriſt the firſt-fruits; afterward they that are Chriſt's, at his coming. Then cometh the end when he ſhall have delivered up the kingdom to God even the Father; when he ſhall have put down all rule and all authority and power: for he muſt reign till he hath put all enemies under his feet. The laſt enemy that ſhall be deſtroyed is death: for he hath put all things under his feet. But when he ſaith all things are put under him, it is manifeſt that he is excepted who did put all things under him. And when all things ſhall be ſubdued unto him, then ſhall the Son alſo himſelf be ſubject unto him that put all things under him, that God may be all in all. Elſe what ſhall they do who are baptized for the dead, if the dead riſe not at all? Why are they then baptized for the dead? and why ſtand we in jeopardy every hour? I proteſt by your rejoicing, which I have in Chriſt Jeſus our Lord, I die daily. If after the manner of men I have fought with beaſts at Epheſus, what advantageth it me, if the dead riſe not? Let us eat and drink for to-morrow we die. Be not deceived: evil communications corrupt good manners. Awake to righteouſneſs, and ſin not: for ſome have not the knowledge of God. I ſpeak this to your ſhame But ſome man will ſay, How are the dead raiſed up?

up? and with what body do they come? Thou fool, that which thou foweſt is not quickened, except it die. And that which thou foweſt, thou foweſt not that body that ſhall be, but bare grain, it may chance of wheat, or of ſome other grain: But God giveth it a body as it hath pleaſed him, and to every ſeed his own body. All fleſh is not the ſame fleſh : but there is one kind of fleſh of men, another fleſh of beaſts, another of fiſhes, and another of birds. There are alſo celeſtial bodies, and bodies terreſtrial : but the glory of the celeſtial is one, and the glory of the terreſtrial is another. There is one glory of the ſun, and another glory of the moon, and another glory of the ſtars : for one ſtar differeth from another ſtar in glory. So alſo is the reſurrection of the dead. It is ſown in corruption ; it is raiſed in incorruption : it is ſown in diſhonour, it is raiſed in glory : it is ſown in weakneſs ; it is raiſed in power : it is ſown a natural body, it is raiſed a ſpiritual body. There is a natural body, and there is a ſpiritual body. And fo it is written, The firſt man Adam was made a living ſoul ; the laſt Adam was made a quickening ſpirit. Howbeit that was not firſt which is ſpiritual, but that which is natural ; and afterward that which is ſpiritual. The firſt man is of the earth, earthy ; the ſecond man is the Lord from heaven. As is the earthy, ſuch are they that are earthy : and as is the heavenly, ſuch are they alſo that are heavenly. And as we have borne the image of the earthy, we ſhall alſo bear the image of the heavenly. Now this I ſay, brethren, that fleſh and blood cannot inherit the kingdom of God ; neither doth corruption inherit incorruption. Behold, I ſhew you a myſtery ; We ſhall not all ſleep, but we ſhall all be changed, in a moment, in the twinkling of an eye, at the laſt trump : For the trumpet ſhall ſound, and the dead ſhall be raiſed

I                                        incorruptible,

incorruptible, and we fhall be changed. For this corruptible muft put on incorruption, and this mortal muft put on immortality. So when this corruptible fhall have put on incorruption, and this mortal fhall have put on immortality, then fhall be brought to pafs the faying that is written. Death is fwallowed up in victory. O death, where is thy fting? O grave, where is thy victory? The fting of death is fin, and the ftrength of fin is the law. But thanks be to God, who giveth us the victory, through our Lord Jefus Chrift. Therefore, my beloved brethren, be ye ftedfaft, immoveable, always abounding in the work of the Lord; forafmuch as ye know that your labour is not in vain in the Lord.

*At the Grave, when the Corpfe is laid in the earth, the Minifter fhall fay,*

MAN that is born of a woman hath but a fhort time to live, and is full of mifery. He cometh up, and is cut down like a flower; he fleeth as it were a fhadow, and never continueth in one ftay.

In the midft of life we are in death; of whom may we feek for fuccour, but of thee, O Lord, who for our fins art juftly difpleafed?

Yet, O Lord God moft holy, O Lord moft mighty, O holy and moft merciful Saviour, deliver us not into the bitter pains of eternal death.

Thou knoweft, Lord, the fecrets of our hearts: fhut not thy merciful ears to our prayers; but fpare us, Lord moft holy, O God moft mighty, O holy and merciful Saviour, thou moft worthy Judge eternal, fuffer us not at our laft hour for any pains of death to fall from thee.

*Then fhall be faid,*

I Heard a voice from heaven, faying unto me, Write; From henceforth bleffed are the dead who die in the Lord: even fo faith the Spirit; for they reft from their labours.

2

*Then*

*Then shall the Minister say,*

Lord, have mercy upon us.

*Christ, have mercy upon us.*

Lord, have mercy upon us.

OUR Father, who art in heaven, Hallowed be thy Name; Thy kingdom come; Thy will be done on earth, as it is in heaven : Give us this day our daily bread ; And forgive us our trespasses, as we forgive them that trespass against us ; And lead us not into temptation ; But deliver us from evil. *Amen.*

## The Collect.

O Merciful God, the Father of our Lord Jesus Christ, who is the resurrection and the life ; in whom whosoever believeth shall live, though he die : and whosoever liveth and believeth in him, shall not die eternally : We meekly beseech thee, O Father, to raise us from the death of sin unto the life of righteousness ; that when we shall depart this life, we may rest in him ; and at the general resurrection on the last day, may be found acceptable in thy sight, and receive that blessing which thy well-beloved Son shall then pronounce to all that love and fear thee, saying, Come, ye blessed children of my Father, receive the kingdom prepared for you from the beginning of the world. Grant this, we beseech thee, O merciful Father, through Jesus Christ our Mediator and Redeemer. *Amen.*

THE grace of our Lord Jesus Christ, and the love of God, and the fellowship of the Holy Ghost, be with us all evermore. *Amen.*

# SELECT PSALMS

[*Ed. Note:* This section comprises pages 166-284 in Wesley's 1784 book. The versification is based on the King James version]

## THE FIRST DAY
*Morning Prayer:*
Psalm 1:1-6
Psalm 2:1-12
*Evening Prayer:*
Psalm 3:1-8
Psalm 4:1-8
Psalm 5:1-8, 11-12

## THE SECOND DAY
*Morning Prayer:*
Psalm 6:1-10
Psalm 7:1-15, 17
*Evening Prayer:*
Psalm 8:1-9
Psalm 9:1-20

## THE THIRD DAY
*Morning Prayer:*
Psalm 10:1-5, 12-18
Psalm 11:1-7
Psalm 12:1-8
*Evening Prayer:*
Psalm 13:1-6
Psalm 15:1-5
Psalm 16:1-11

## THE FOURTH DAY
*Morning Prayer:*
Psalm 17:1-8, 13-15
Psalm 18:1-24
*Evening Prayer:*
Psalm 18:28, 30-36, 46-49.
Psalm 19:1-14

## THE FIFTH DAY
*Morning Prayer:*
Psalm 20:1-2, 5-9
Psalm 22 (Part 1) 1-11, 14-15, 16c-21

*Evening Prayer:*
Psalm 22 (Part 2) 22-28, 29b-31
Psalm 23:1-6
Psalm 24:1-10

## THE SIXTH DAY
*Morning Prayer:*
Psalm 25:1-18, 20
Psalm 26:1-9, 11-12
*Evening Prayer:*
Psalm 27:1-14
Psalm 28:1-3, 6-9

## THE SEVENTH DAY
*Morning Prayer:*
Psalm 29:1-11
Psalm 30:1-12
*Evening Prayer:*
Psalm 31:1-5, 7-8, 14-16, 19-20, 23-24
Psalm 32:1-11

## THE EIGHTH DAY
*Morning Prayer:*
Psalm 33:1, 3-22
*Evening Prayer:*
Psalm 34:1-22
Psalm 35:1-2, 10, 18, 27-28

## THE NINTH DAY
*Morning Prayer:*
Psalm 36:5-12
Psalm 37:1-13, 16-22
*Evening Prayer:*
Psalm 37:23-40
Psalm 38:1-6, 8-11, 15, 18, 21-22

## THE TENTH DAY
*Morning Prayer:*
Psalm 39:1-13
Psalm 40:1-13, 16-17
*Evening Prayer:*
Psalm 41:1-4, 11-13
Psalm 42:1-5, 8-9, 11
Psalm 43:1-5

## THE ELEVENTH DAY
*Morning Prayer:*
Psalm 44:1-8
Psalm 45:1-7, 17
Psalm 46:1-11
*Evening Prayer:*
Psalm 47:1-8, 9b
Psalm 48:1-8, 14
Psalm 49:1-3, 6-20

## THE TWELFTH DAY
*Morning Prayer:*
Psalm 50:1-17, 22-23
Psalm 51:1-17
*Evening Prayer:*
Psalm 55:1-2, 4-8, 12-14, 16-19,
    22-23
Psalm 56:1, 3-4, 9-13

## THE THIRTEENTH DAY
*Morning Prayer:*
Psalm 57:1-2, 5, 7, 9-11
Psalm 59:1-2, 9-10, 16-17
Psalm 61:1-5, 8
Psalm 62:1-2, 5-12
*Evening Prayer:*
Psalm 63:1-8
Psalm 65:1-13

## THE FOURTEENTH DAY
*Morning Prayer:*
Psalm 66:1-14, 16-20
Psalm 67:1-6
*Evening Prayer:*
Psalm 68:1-10, 18-20, 28, 32-34
Psalm 69:1-3, 6-10, 13-21, 29-30,
    32-34

## THE FIFTEENTH DAY
Morning Prayer:
Psalm 70:1, 4-5
Psalm 71:1-9, 12, 14-21, 23-24a
*Evening Prayer:*
Psalm 73:1-3, 16-26
Psalm 75:1-2, 4-10

## THE SIXTEENTH DAY
*Morning Prayer:*
Psalm 76:7-12
Psalm 77:1-20
*Evening Prayer:*
Psalm 84:1-12
Psalm 85:1-13

## THE SEVENTEENTH DAY
*Morning Prayer:*
Psalm 86:1-13, 15-17
Psalm 89:1-9, 11, 13-18
*Evening Prayer:*
Psalm 90:1-17
Psalm 91:1-16

## THE EIGHTEENTH DAY
*Morning Prayer:*
Psalm 92:1-2, 4-9, 12-15
Psalm 93:1-5
*Evening Prayer:*
Psalm 95:1-11
Psalm 96:1-13

## THE NINETEENTH DAY
*Morning Prayer:*
Psalm 97:1-6, 9-12
Psalm 98:1-4, 7-9
Psalm 99:1-3, 5, 9
*Evening Prayer:*
Psalm 100:1-5
Psalm 102:1-28

## THE TWENTIETH DAY
*Morning Prayer:*
Psalm 103:1-22
*Evening Prayer:*
Psalm 104:1-35

[199-244]

## THE TWENTY-FIRST DAY
*Morning Prayer:*
Psalm 107:1-22
*Evening Prayer:*
Psalm 107:23-43

## THE TWENTY-SECOND DAY
*Morning Prayer:*
Psalm 111:1-5, 7-10
Psalm 112:1-7, 9-10
Psalm 113:1-9
*Evening Prayer:*
Psalm 114:1-8
Psalm 115:1-3, 9-18

## THE TWENTY-THIRD DAY
*Morning Prayer:*
Psalm 116:1-19
Psalm 117:1-2
*Evening Prayer:*
Psalm 118:1-29

## THE TWENTY-FOURTH DAY
*Morning Prayer:*
Psalm 119:1-32
*Evening Prayer:*
Psalm 119:33-64

## THE TWENTY-FIFTH DAY
*Morning Prayer:*
Psalm 119:65-96
*Evening Prayer:*
Psalm 119:97-128

## THE TWENTY-SIXTH DAY
*Morning Prayer:*
Psalm 119:129-160
*Evening Prayer:*
Psalm 119:161-176
Psalm 121:1-8

## THE TWENTY-SEVENTH DAY
*Morning Prayer:*
Psalm 123:1-4
Psalm 124:1-8
Psalm 125:1-5
Psalm 126:1-6
*Evening Prayer:*
Psalm 127:1-6
Psalm 128:1-6
Psalm 130:1-8
Psalm 131:1-3
Psalm 133:1-3

## THE TWENTY-EIGHTH DAY
*Morning Prayer:*
Psalm 135:1-7, 13-14, 19-21
Psalm 138:1-8
*Evening Prayer:*
Psalm 139:1-18, 23-24

## THE TWENTY-NINTH DAY
*Morning Prayer:*
Psalm 141:1-5c, 8-9
Psalm 142:1-7
*Evening Prayer:*
Psalm 143:1-2, 4-11
Psalm 144:1-9a, 10-15

## THE THIRTIETH DAY
*Morning Prayer:*
Psalm 145:1-21
Psalm 146:1-10
*Evening Prayer:*
Psalm 147:1-7a, 8-20
Psalm 148:1-14
Psalm 150:1-2, 6

THE END OF THE PSALMS

## The Form and Manner of Making and Ordaining of SUPERINTENDANTS, ELDERS, and DEACONS.

### The Form and Manner of making of DEACONS.

*When the Day appointed by the Superintendant is come, after Morning Prayer is ended, there shall be a Sermon, or Exhortation, declaring the Duty and Office of such as come to be admitted Deacons.*

*After which one of the Elders shall present unto the Superintendant the Persons to be ordained Deacons: and their Names being read aloud, the Superintendant shall say unto the People:*

BRethren, if there be any of you, who knoweth any impediment or crime in any of these persons presented to be ordained deacons, for the which he ought not to be admitted to that office, let him come forth in the Name of God, and shew what the crime or impediment is.

*And if any Crime or Impediment be objected, the Superintendant shall surcease from ordaining that Person, until such Time as the Party accused shall be found clear of that Crime.*

*Then the Superintendant (commending such as shall be found meet to be ordained, to the Prayers of the Congregation) shall, with the Ministers and People present, say the Litany.*

*Then*

*Then ſhall be ſaid the Service for the Communion, with the Collect, Epiſtle, and Goſpel, as followeth.*

### The Collect.

ALmighty God, who by thy Divine Providence haſt appointed divers orders of miniſters in thy church, and didſt inſpire thine apoſtles to chooſe into the order of deacons the firſt martyr Saint Stephen, with others ; Mercifully behold theſe thy ſervants now called to the like office and adminiſtration ; repleniſh them ſo with the truth of thy doctrine, and adorn them with innocency of life, that both by word and good example they may faithfully ſerve thee in this office, to the glory of thy Name, and the edification of thy church, through the merits of our Saviour Jeſus Chriſt, who liveth and reigneth with thee and the Holy Ghoſt, now and for ever. *Amen.*

### The Epiſtle. 1 Tim. iii. 8.

LIkewiſe muſt the Deacons be grave, not double-tongued, not given to much wine, not greedy of filthy lucre ; holding the myſtery of the faith in a pure conſcience. And let theſe alſo firſt be proved ; then let them uſe the office of a deacon, being found blameleſs. Even ſo muſt their wives be grave, not ſlanderers, ſober, faithful in all things. Let the deacons be the huſbands of one wife, ruling their children and their own houſes well. For they that have uſed the office of a deacon well, purchaſe to themſelves a good degree, and great boldneſs in the faith which is in Chriſt Jeſus.

*Then*

*Then ſhall the Superintendant examine every one of them that are to be ordained, in the Preſence of the People, after this manner following :*

DO you truſt that you are inwardly moved by the Holy Ghoſt to take upon you this office and miniſtration, to ſerve God for the promoting of his glory, and the edifying of his people ?

*Anſwer.* I truſt ſo.

### The Superintendant.

DO you think that you are truly called, according to the will of our Lord Jeſus Chriſt, to the miniſtry of the church ?

*Anſwer.* I think ſo.

### The Superintendant.

DO you unfeignedly believe all the canonical Scriptures of the Old and New Teſtament ?

*Anſwer.* I do believe them.

### The Superintendant.

WILL you diligently read the ſame unto the people whom you ſhall be appointed to ſerve ?

*Anſwer.* I will.

### The Superintendant.

IT appertaineth to the office of a Deacon, to aſſiſt the elder in Divine Service, and eſpecially when he miniſtereth the holy Communion, to help him in the diſtribution thereof, and to read and expound the holy Scriptures; to inſtruct the youth, and in the abſence of the elder to baptize. And furthermore, it is his office, to ſearch for the ſick, poor,
and

and impotent, that they may be vifited and relieved. Will you do this gladly and willingly?

*Anfwer.* I will do fo, by the help of God.

### *The Superintendant.*

WILL you apply all your diligence to frame and fafhion your own lives, and the lives of your families, according to the doctrine of Chrift; and to make both yourfelves and them, as much as in you lieth, wholfome examples of the flock of Chrift?

*Anfwer.* I will fo do, the Lord being my helper.

### *The Superintendant.*

WILL you reverently obey them to whom the charge and government over you is committed, following with a glad mind and will their godly admonitions?

*Anfwer.* I will endeavour fo to do, the Lord being my helper.

*Then the Superintendant laying his Hands feverally upon the Head of every one of them fhall fay,*

TAKE thou authority to execute the office of a deacon in the church of God; In the Name of the Father, and of the Son, and of the Holy Ghoft. *Amen.*

*Then fhall the Superintendant deliver to every one of them the Holy Bible, faying,*

TAKE thou authority to read the holy Scriptures in the church of God, and to preach the fame.

Then

*Then one of them appointed by the Superintendant*
*shall read,*

### The Gospel. Luke, xii. 35.

LET your loins be girded about, and your lights
burning, and ye yourselves like unto men that
wait for their Lord, when he will return from the
wedding, that when he cometh and knocketh,
they may open unto him immediately. Blessed are
those servants, whom the Lord when he cometh
shall find watching. Verily I say unto you, That
he shall gird himself, and make them to sit down to
meat, and will come forth and serve them. And
if he shall come in the second watch, or come in
the third watch, and find them so, blessed are those
servants.

*Then shall the Superintendant proceed in the Commu-*
*nion, and all that are ordained shall receive the holy*
*Communion.*

*The Communion ended, immediately before the Bene-*
*diction, shall be said these Collects following :*

ALmighty God, giver of all good things, who
of thy great goodness hast vouchsafed to accept and take these thy servants into the office of
deacons in thy church ; Make them, we beseech
thee, O Lord, to be modest, humble, and constant in their ministration, and to have a ready
will to observe all spiritual discipline ; that they
having always the testimony of a good conscience,
and continuing ever stable and strong in thy Son
Christ, may so well behave themselves in this inferior office, that they may be found worthy to
be called unto the higher ministries in thy church,
through the same thy Son our Saviour Jesus Christ ;

to

to whom be glory and honour world without end. *Amen.*

PRevent us, O Lord, in all our doings with thy moft gracious favour, and further us with thy continual help; that in all our works begun, continued, and ended in thee, we may glorify thy holy Name, and finally by thy mercy, obtain everlafting life, through Jefus Chrift our Lord. *Amen.*

THE peace of God, which paffeth all underftanding, keep your hearts and minds in the knowledge and love of God, and of his Son Jefus Chrift our Lord. And the bleffing of God Almighty, the Father, the Son, and the Holy Ghoft, be amongft you, and remain with you always. *Amen.*

---

## The Form and Manner of ordaining of ELDERS.

*When the Day appointed by the Superintendant is come, after Morning Prayer is ended, there ſhall be a Sermon or Exhortation, declaring the Duty and Office of ſuch as come to be admitted Elders ; how neceſſary that Order is in the Church of Chriſt, and alſo how the People ought to eſteem them in their Office.*

*Firſt, one of the Elders ſhall preſent unto the Superintendant all them that are to be ordained, and ſay,*

I Prefent unto you thefe perfons prefent, to be ordained Elders.

*Then*

*Then their Names being read aloud, the Superin-*
*tendant ſhall ſay unto the People ;*

GOOD People, theſe are they whom we pur-
poſe, God willing, this day to ordain Elders.
For after due examination, we find not to the contrary, but that they are lawfully called to this
function and miniſtry, and that they are perſons
meet for the ſame. But if there be any of you,
who knoweth any impediment or crime in any of
them, for the which he ought not to be received
into this holy miniſtry, let him come forth in the
name of God, and ſhew what the crime or impediment is.

*And if any Crime or Impediment be objected, the Super-*
*intendant ſhall ſurceaſe from ordaining that Perſon,*
*until ſuch Time as the Party accuſed ſhall be found*
*clear of that Crime.*

*Then the Superintendant (commending ſuch as ſhall be*
*found meet to be ordained, to the Prayers of the*
*Congregation) ſhall, with the Miniſters and People*
*preſent, ſay the Litany, as is before appointed in the*
*Form of Ordaining Deacons, omitting the laſt*
*Prayer, and the Bleſſing.*

*Then ſhall be ſaid the Service for the Communion ;*
*with the Collect, Epiſtle, and Goſpel, as followeth.*

### The Collect.

ALmighty God, giver of all good things, who
by thy holy Spirit haſt appointed divers orders
of miniſters in thy church ; mercifully behold theſe
thy ſervants now called to the office of Elders ;
and repleniſh them ſo with the truth of thy doctrine, and adorn them with innocency of life, that
both by word and good example they may faithfully ſerve thee in this office, to the glory of thy
name, and the edification of thy church, through
the

the merits of our Saviour Jefus Chrift, who liveth and reigneth, with thee and the Holy Ghoft, world without end. *Amen.*

### *The Epiftle.* Ephef. iv. 7.

UNto every one of us is given grace according to the meafure of the gift of Chrift. Wherefore he faith, When he afcended up on high, he led captivity captive, and gave gifts unto men. (Now that he afcended, what is it but that he alfo defcended firft into the lower parts of the earth? He that defcended, is the fame alfo that afcended up far above all things.) And he gave fome Apoftles, and fome prophets, and fome evangelifts, and fome paftors and teachers, for the perfecting of the faints, for the work of the miniftry, for the edifying of the body of Chrift; till we all come in the unity of the faith, and of the knowledge of the Son of God, unto a perfect man, unto the meafure of the ftature of the fulnefs of Chrift.

*After this fhall be read for the Gofpel, part of the Tenth Chapter of Saint John.*

### S. *John*, x. 1.

VErily verily I fay unto you, He that entereth not by the door into the fheep-fold, but climbeth up fome other way, the fame is a thief and a robber. But he that entereth in by the door, is the fhepherd of the fheep. To him the porter openeth, and the fheep hear his voice; and he calleth his own fheep by name, and leadeth them out. And when he putteth forth his own fheep, he goeth before them, and the fheep follow him; for they know his voice. And a ftranger will they not follow, but flee from him; for they know not the voice of ftrangers. This parable fpake Jefus unto them, but they underftood not what things
they

they were which he fpake unto them. Then faid
Jefus unto them again, Verily verily I fay unto
you, I am the door of the fheep. All that ever
came before me are thieves and robbers ; but the
fheep did not hear them. I am the door ; by me
if any man enter in, he fhall be faved, and fhall
go in and out, and find pafture. The thief
cometh not but for to fteal, and to kill, and to
deftroy : I am come that they might have life, and
that they might have it more abundantly. I am
the good Shepherd : the good Shepherd giveth his
life for the fheep. But he that is an hireling, and
not the Shepherd, whofe own the fheep are not,
feeth the wolf coming, and leaveth the fheep, and
fleeth ; and the wolf catcheth them, and fcattereth
the fheep. The hireling fleeth becaufe he is an
hireling, and careth not for the fheep. I am the
good Shepherd, and know my fheep, and am
known of mine. As the Father knoweth me,
even fo know I the Father : and I lay down my
life for the fheep. And other fheep I have, which
are not of this fold : them alfo I muft bring, and
they fhall hear my voice ; and there fhall be one
fold, and one Shepherd.

*And that done, the Superintendant fhall fay unto them
as hereafter followeth,*

YOU have heard, brethren, as well in your private examination, as in the exhortation which
was now made to you, and in the holy leffons taken
out of the Gofpel, and the writings of the Apoftles,
of what dignity, and of how great importance this
office is, whereunto ye are called. And now
again we exhort you in the name of our Lord Jefus
Chrift, that you have in remembrance, into how
high a dignity, and to how weighty an office and
charge ye are called : That is to fay, to be Meffen-
gers, watchmen, and ftewards of the Lord ; to
teach

teach, and to premonifh, to feed and provide for the Lord's family ; to feek for Chrift's fheep that are difperfed abroad, and for his children who are in the midft of this naughty world, that they may be faved through Chrift for ever.

Have always therefore printed in your remembrance, how great a treafure is committed to your charge. For they are the fheep of Chrift, which he bought with his death, and for whom he fhed his blood. The church and congregation whom you muft ferve, is his Spoufe, and his body. And if it fhall happen, the fame church, or any member thereof do take any hurt or hindrance by reafon of your negligence, ye know the greatnefs of the fault, and alfo the horrible punifhment that will enfue. Wherefore confider with yourfelves the end of the miniftry towards the children of God, towards the fpoufe and body of Chrift ; and fee that you never ceafe your labour, your care and diligence, until you have done all that lieth in you, according to your bounden duty, to bring all fuch as are or fhall be committed to your charge, unto that agreement in the faith and knowledge of God, and to that ripenefs and perfectnefs of age in Chrift, that there be no place left among you, either for error in religion, or for vicioufnefs in life.

Forafmuch then as your office is both of fo great excellency, and of fo great difficulty, ye fee with how great care and ftudy ye ought to apply yourfelves, as well that ye may fhew yourfelves dutiful and thankful unto that Lord, who hath placed you in fo high a dignity ; as alfo to beware that neither you yourfelves offend, nor be occafion that others offend. Howbeit ye cannot have a mind and will thereto of yourfelves ; for that will and ability is given of God alone : therefore ye ought, and have need to pray earneftly for his holy Spirit. And feeing that you cannot by any other means

N compafs

compafs the doing of fo weighty a work, pertaining to the falvation of man, but with doctrine and
exhortation taken out of the Holy Scriptures, and
with a life agreeable to the fame: confider how
ftudious ye ought to be in reading and learning the
Scriptures, and in framing the manners both of
yourfelves, and of them that fpecially pertain unto
you, according to the rule of the fame Scriptures:
and for this felf-fame caufe, how ye ought to for-
fake and fet afide (as much as you may) all worldly
cares and ftudies.

We have good hope that you have all weighed
and pondered thefe things with yourfelves long
before this time; and that you have clearly determined, by God's grace, to give yourfelves wholly
to this office, whereunto it hath pleafed God to
call you: fo that, as much as lieth in you, you
will apply yourfelves wholly to this one thing, and
draw all your cares and ftudies this way, and that
you will continually pray to God the Father, by
the mediation of our only Saviour Jefus Chrift, for
the heavenly affiftance of the Holy Ghoft; that by
daily reading and weighing of the Scriptures, ye
may wax riper and ftronger in your miniftry; and
that ye may fo endeavour yourfelves from time to
time to fanctify the lives of you and your's, and to
fafhion them after the rule and doctrine of Chrift,
that ye may be wholefome and godly examples
and patterns for the people to follow.

And now that this prefent congregation of Chrift,
here affembled, may alfo underftand your minds
and wills in thefe things, and that this your promife may the more move you to do your duties; ye
fhall anfwer plainly to thefe things, which we, in
the Name of God, and of his Church, fhall demand of you touching the fame.

**Do**

DO you think in your heart, that you are truly called, according to the will of our Lord Jefus Chrift, to the order of Elders.

*Anfwer.* I think fo.

### The Superintendant.

ARE you perfuaded that the Holy Scriptures contain fufficiently all doctrine required of neceffity for eternal falvation through faith in Jefus Chrift? And are you determined, out of the faid Scriptures to inftruct the people committed to your charge, and to teach nothing, as required of neceffity to eternal falvation, but that which you fhall be perfuaded, may be concluded and proved by the Scripture?

*Anfwer.* I am fo perfuaded, and have fo determined, by God's grace.

### The Superintendant.

WILL you then give your faithful diligence, always fo to minifter the doctrine and facraments, and the difcipline of Chrift, as the Lord hath commanded.

*Anfwer.* I will fo do, by the help of the Lord.

### The Superintendant.

WILL you be ready with all faithful diligence to banifh and drive away all erroneous and ftrange doctrines contrary to God's word; and to ufe both public and private monitions and exhortations, as well to the fick as to the whole within your diftrict, as need fhall require, and occafion fhall be given?

*Anfwer.* I will, the Lord being my helper.

N 2 *The*

### The Superintendant.

WILL you be diligent in prayers, and in reading of the holy Scriptures, and in such studies
as help to the knowledge of the same, laying aside
the study of the world and the flesh.

*Answer.* I will endeavour so to do, the Lord
being my helper.

### The Superintendant.

WILL you be diligent to frame and fashion your
own selves, and your families, according to
the doctrine of Christ; and to make both yourselves and them, as much as in you lieth, wholesome examples and patterns to the flock of Christ?

*Answer.* I shall apply myself thereto, the Lord
being my helper.

### The Superintendant.

WILL you maintain and set forwards, as much
as lieth in you, quietness, peace and love
among all Christian people, and especially among
them that are or shall be committed to your
charge?

*Answer.* I will do so, the Lord being my helper.

### The Superintendant.

WILL you reverently obey your chief ministers, unto whom is committed the charge
and government over you; following with a glad
mind and will their godly admonitions, and sub-
mitting yourselves to their godly judgments?

*Answer.* I will so do, the Lord being my helper.

*Then shall the Superintendant standing up, say,*

ALmighty God, who hath given you this will
to do all these things; grant also unto you
strength and power to perform the same; that he
may

may accomplish his work which he hath begun in you, through Jesus Christ our Lord. *Amen.*

*After this the Congregation shall be desired, secretly in their Prayers, to make their humble Supplications to God for all these Things: for the which Prayers there shall be Silence kept for a Space.*

*After which shall be said by the Superintendant (the Persons to be ordained Elders, all kneeling) V*eni, *Creator, Spiritus ; the Superintendant beginning, and the Elders and others that are present answering by Verses, as followeth.*

COme, Holy Ghoft, our souls inspire,
  *And lighten with celeftial fire.*
Thou the anointing Spirit art,
*Who doft thy sev'nfold gifts impart :*
Thy bleffed Unction from above,
*Is comfort, life, and fire of love.*
Enable with perpetual light,
*The dulnefs of our blinded fight :*
Anoint and cheer our foiled face
*With the abundance of thy grace :*
Keep far our foes, give peace at home ;
*Where thou art Guide no ill can come.*
Teach us to know the Father, Son,
*And thee of both, to be but one :*
That through the ages all along,
*This may be our endlefs Song ;*
Praife to thy eternal merit,
*Father, Son, and Holy Spirit.*

*That done, the Superintendant shall pray in this wise, and say,*

Let us pray.

ALmighty God, and heavenly Father, who of thine infinite love and goodnefs towards us, haft given to us thy only and moft dearly beloved
Son

Son Jefus Chrift to be our Redeemer, and the Author of everlafting life ; who after he had made perfect our redemption by his death, and was afcended into heaven, fent abroad into the world his Apoftles, Prophets, Evangelifts, Doctors, and Paftors ; by whofe labour and miniftry he gathered together a great flock in all the parts of the world, to fet forth the eternal praife of thy holy Name : for thefe fo great benefits of thy eternal goodnefs, and for that thou haft vouchfafed to call thefe thy fervants here prefent to the fame Office and Miniftry appointed for the falvation of mankind, we render unto thee moft hearty thanks, we praife and worfhip thee ; and we humbly befeech thee by the fame thy bleffed Son, to grant unto all, who either here or elfewhere call upon thy holy Name, that we may continue to fhew ourfelves thankful unto thee for thefe and all other thy benefits ; and that we may daily increafe and go forwards in the knowledge and faith of thee and thy Son by the Holy Spirit. So that as well by thefe thy Minifters, as by them over whom they fhall be appointed thy Minifters, thy holy Name may be for ever glorified, and thy bleffed kingdom enlarged, through the fame thy Son Jefus Chrift our Lord; who liveth and reigneth with thee in the unity of the fame Holy Spirit, world without end. *Amen.*

*When this Prayer is done, the Superintendant, with the Elders prefent, fhall lay their hands feverally upon the Head of every one that receiveth the order of Elders : the Receivers humbly kneeling upon their knees, and the Superintendant faying,*

R Eceive the Holy Ghoft for the Office and Work of an Elder in the Church of God, now committed unto thee by the impofition of our hands. And be thou a faithful Difpenfer of the Word of God, and of his holy Sacraments ; in the Name
of

of the Father, and of the Son, and of the Holy
Ghoſt. *Amen.*

*Then the Superintendant ſhall deliver to every one of
them, kneeling, the Bible into his hand, ſaying,*

TAKE thou authority to preach the Word of
God, and to adminiſter the holy Sacraments
in the Congregation.

*When this is done, the Superintendant ſhall go on in the
Service of the Communion, which all they that receive Orders ſhall take together.*

*The Communion being done, after the laſt Collect, and
immediately before the Benediction, ſhall be ſaid theſe
Collects.*

MOST merciful Father, we beſeech thee to
ſend upon theſe thy ſervants thy heavenly
bleſſing; that they may be clothed with righteouſneſs, and thy Word ſpoken by their mouths, may
have ſuch ſucceſs, that it may never be ſpoken in
vain. Grant alſo, that we may have grace to hear
and receive what they ſhall deliver out of thy moſt
holy Word, or agreeable to the ſame, as the means
of our ſalvation; that in all our words and deeds
we may ſeek thy glory, and the increaſe of thy
kingdom, through Jeſus Chriſt our Lord. *Amen.*

PRevent us, O Lord, in all our doings, with thy
moſt gracious favour, and further us with thy
continual help; that in all our works begun, continued, and ended in thee, we may glorify thy
holy Name, and finally by thy mercy obtain everlaſting life, through Jeſus Chriſt our Lord. *Amen.*

THE Peace of God, which paſſeth all underſtanding, keep your hearts and minds in the
knowledge and love of God, and of his Son Jeſus
Chriſt our Lord : and the bleſſing of God Almighty

the

the Father, the Son, and the Holy Ghoft, be amongft you, and remain with you always. *Amen.*

*And if on the fame day the Order of Deacons be given to fome, and that of Elders to others; the Deacons fhall be firft prefented, and then the Elders; and it fhall fuffice, that the Litany be once faid for both. The Collects fhall both be ufed; firft, that for Deacons, then that for Elders. The Epiftle fhall be* Ephef. iv. 7. *to* 13. *as before in this Office. Immediately after which, they that are to be ordained Deacons fhall be examined, and ordained, as is above prefcribed. Then one of them having read the Gofpel, which fhall be* St. John, x. 1. *as before in this Office; they that are to be ordained Elders, fhall likewife be examined and ordained, as is in this Office before appointed.*

---

## The Form of Ordaining of a SUPERINTENDANT.

*After Morning Prayer is ended, the Superintendant fhall begin the Communion Service; in which this fhall be*

### The Collect.

ALmighty God, who by thy Son Jefus Chrift didft give to thy holy Apoftles many excellent gifts, and didft charge them to feed thy flock; give grace, we befeech thee, to all the Minifters and Paftors of thy Church, that they may diligently preach thy Word, and duly adminifter the godly Difcipline thereof; and grant to the people, that they may obediently follow the fame; that all may receive the crown of everlafting glory, through Jefus Chrift our Lord. *Amen.*

*Then*

*Then shall be read by one of the Elders, the Epistle.*
Acts, xx. 17.

FROM Miletus Paul sent to Ephesus, and called the Elders of the Church. And when they were come to him, he said unto them, Ye know from the first day that I came into Asia, after what manner I have been with you at all seasons, serving the Lord with all humility of mind, and with many tears and temptations, which befel me by the lying in wait of the Jews : and how I kept back nothing that was profitable unto you, but have shewed you, and have taught you publickly, and from house to house, testifying both to the Jews, and also to the Greeks, repentance toward God, and faith toward our Lord Jesus Christ. And now behold, I go bound in the Spirit unto Jerusalem, not knowing the things that shall befal me there; save that the Holy Ghost witnesseth in every city, saying, That bonds and afflictions abide me. But none of these things move me, neither count I my life dear unto myself, so that I might finish my course with joy, and the ministry which I have received of the Lord Jesus ; to testify the Gospel of the grace of God. And now, behold, I know that ye all, among whom I have gone preaching the Kingdom of God, shall see my face no more. Wherefore I take you to record this day, that I am pure from the blood of all men. For I have not shunned to declare unto you all the counsel of God. Take heed therefore unto yourselves, and to all the flock, over the which the Holy Ghost hath made you Overseers, to feed the Church of God, which he hath purchased with his own blood. For I know this, that after my departing shall grievous wolves enter in among you, not sparing the flock. Also of your own selves shall men arise, speaking perverse things, to draw away disciples after them.

N 5                                    Therefore

Therefore watch, and remember, that by the fpace of three years, I ceafed not to warn every one night and day with tears. And now, brethren, I commend you to God, and to the word of his grace, which is able to build you up, and to give you an inheritance among them who are fanctified. I have coveted no man's filver, or gold, or apparel : yea, ye yourfelves know, that thefe hands have miniftered unto my neceffities, and to them that were with me. I have fhewed you all things, how that fo labouring ye ought to fupport the weak ; and to remember the words of the Lord Jefus, how he faid, It is more bleffed to give than to receive.

*Then another Elder fhall read,*

*The Gofpel,* St. John, xxi. 15.

JESUS faith to Simon Peter, Simon, fon of Jonas loveft thou me more than thefe ? He faith unto him, Yea, Lord; thou knoweft that I love thee. He faid unto him, Feed my lambs. He faith to him again the fecond time, Simon, fon of Jonas, loveft thou me ? He faith unto him, Yea, Lord ; thou knoweft that I love thee. He faith unto him, Feed my fheep. He faith unto him the third time, Simon, fon of Jonas, loveft thou me ? Peter was grieved becaufe he faid unto him the third time, Loveft thou me ? And he faid unto him, Lord, thou knoweft all things : thou knoweft that I love thee. Jefus faith unto him, Feed my fheep.

*Or this :* St. Matth. xxviii. 18.

JESUS came and fpake unto them, faying, All power is given unto me in heaven and in earth. Go ye therefore and teach all nations, baptizing them, In the Name of the Father, and of the Son, and of the Holy Ghoft ; teaching them to obferve
all

all things whatfoever I have commanded you; and lo, I am with you alway, even unto the end of the world.

*After the Gofpel and the Sermon are ended, the elected Perfon fhall be prefented by two Elders unto the Superintendant, faying,*

WE prefent unto you this godly Man to be ordained a Superintendant.

*Then the Superintendant fhall move the Congregation prefent to pray, faying thus to them:*

BRethren, it is written in the Gofpel of Saint Luke, That our Saviour Chrift continued the whole night in prayer, before he did choofe and fend forth his twelve Apoftles. It is written alfo in the Acts of the Apoftles, That the Difciples who were at Antioch, did faft and pray, before they laid hands on Paul and Barnabas, and fent them forth. Let us therefore, following the example of our Saviour Chrift, and his Apoftles, firft fall to Prayer before we admit, and fend forth this perfon prefented unto us, to the work, whereunto we truft the Holy Ghoft hath called him.

*And then fhall be faid the Litany, as before, in the Form of Ordaining Deacons.*

*Then fhall be faid this Prayer following.*

ALmighty God, giver of all good things, who by thy Holy Spirit haft appointed divers orders of minifters in thy church; mercifully behold this thy fervant now called to the work and miniftry of a Superintendant, and replenifh him fo with the truth of thy doctrine, and adorn him with innocency of life, that, both by word and deed, he may faithfully ferve thee in this office, to the glory of thy Name and the edifying and well-governing of thy church,

N 6

through the merits of our Saviour Jesus Christ, who liveth and reigneth with thee and the Holy Ghost, world without end.  *Amen.*

*Then the Superintendant shall say to him that is to be ordained,*

BRother, forasmuch as the holy Scripture commands that we should not be hasty in laying on hands, and admitting any person to government in the church of Christ, which he hath purchased with no less price than the effusion of his own blood; before I admit you to this administration I will examine you on certain articles, to the end that the congregation present may have a trial, and bear witness how you are minded to behave yourself in the church of God.

ARE you persuaded that you are truly called to this ministration, according to the will of our Lord Jesus Christ?

*Answer.*  I am so persuaded.

### The Superintendant.

ARE you persuaded that the holy Scriptures contain sufficiently all doctrine required of necessity for eternal salvation, through faith in Jesus Christ?    And are you determined out of the same holy Scriptures to instruct the people committed to your charge, and to teach or maintain nothing as required of necessity to eternal salvation, but that which you shall be persuaded may be concluded and proved by the same?

*Answer.*  I am persuaded, and determined by God's grace.

### The Supcrintendant.

WILL you then faithfully exercise yourself in the same holy Scriptures, and call upon God by prayer for the true understanding of the same,

so

fo as you may be able by them to teach and exhort with wholefome doctrine, and to withstand and convince the gainfayers?

*Anfwer.* I will fo do, by the help of God.

### The Superintendant.

ARE you ready, and with faithful diligence, to banish and drive away all erroneous and ftrange doctrines contrary to God's Word, and both privately and openly to call upon and encourage others to the fame?

*Anfwer.* I am ready, the Lord being my helper.

### The Superintendant.

WILL you deny all ungodlinefs and worldly lufts, and live foberly, righteoufly, and godly in this prefent world, that you may fhew yourfelf in all things an example of good works unto others, that the adverfary may be afhamed, having nothing to fay againft you?

*Anfwer.* I will fo do, the Lord being my helper.

### The Superintendant.

WILL you maintain and fet forward, as much as fhall lie in you, quietnefs, love, and peace among all men; and fuch as fhall be unquiet, difobedient, and criminal within your diftrict, correct and punifh, according to fuch authority as you have by God's Word, and as fhall be committed unto you.

*Anfwer.* I will fo do, by the help of God.

### The Superintendant.

WILL you be faithful in ordaining, fending, or laying hands upon others?

*Anfwer.* I will fo be, by the help of God.

The

### The Superintendant.

WILL you fhew yourfelf gentle, and be mer-ciful, for Chrift's fake, to poor and needy people, and to all ftrangers deftitute of help?

*Anfwer.* I will fo fhew myfelf, by God's help.

### Then the Superintendant fhall fay,

ALmighty God, our heavenly Father, who hath given you a good will to do all thefe things, grant alfo unto you ftrength and power to per-form the fame; that, he accomplifhing in you the good work which he hath begun, you may be found perfect and irreprehenfible at the laft day, through Jefus Chrift our Lord. *Amen.*

### Then fhall Veni Creator Spiritus be faid.

COME, Holy Ghoft, our fouls infpire,
  *And lighten with celeftial fire.*
Thou the anointing Spirit art
*Who doft thy fevenfold gifts impart :*
Thy bleffed unction from above
*Is comfort, life, and fire of love.*
Enable with perpetual light
*The dulnefs of our blinded fight.*
Anoint and cheer our foiled face
*With the abundance of thy grace.*
Keep far our foes, give peace at home :
*Where thou art Guide no ill can come.*
Teach us to know the Father, Son,
*And thee of both, to be but one ;*
That through the ages all along,
*This may be our endlefs fong,*
Praife to thy eternal merit,
*Father, Son, and Holy Spirit.*

*That*

*That ended, the Superintendant shall say,*

Lord, hear our prayer.

*Anf.* And let our cry come unto thee.

### Superintendant.
### Let us pray.

ALmighty God and most merciful Father, who of thine infinite goodnefs haft given thine only and dearly beloved Son Jefus Chrift to be our Redeemer, and the Author of everlafting life, who, after that he had made perfe&t our redemption by his death, and was afcended into heaven, poured down his gifts abundantly upon men, making fome Apoftles, fome Prophets, fome Evangelifts, fome Paftors and Do&tors, to the edifying and making perfe&t his church; grant, we befeech thee, to this thy fervant fuch grace, that he may evermore be ready to fpread abroad thy gofpel, the glad tidings of reconciliation with thee, and ufe the authority given him, not to deftru&tion, but to falvation; not to hurt, but to help; fo that, as a wife and faithful fervant, giving to thy Family their portion in due feafon, he may at laft be received into everlafting joy, through Jefus Chrift our Lord, who, with thee and the Holy Ghoft, liveth and reigneth, One God, world without end. *Amen.*

*Then the Superintendant and Elders prefent shall lay their Hands upon the Head of the ele&ted Perfon kneeling before them upon his Knees, the Superintendant faying,*

REceive the Holy Ghoft for the office and work of a Superintendant in the church of God, now committed unto thee by the impofition of our hands, in the Name of the Father, and of the Son,
and

and of the Holy Ghoft. *Amen.* And remember that thou ftir up the grace of God which is given thee by this impofition of our hands ; for God hath not given us the fpirit of fear, but of power, and love, and fobernefs.

*Then the Superintendant ſhall deliver him the Bible, ſaying,*

GIVE heed unto reading, exhortation, and doc-trine. Think upon the things contained in this book. Be diligent in them, that the increafe coming thereby may be manifeft unto all men. Take heed unto thyfelf, and to thy doctrine ; for by fo doing thou fhalt both fave thyfelf and them that hear thee. Be to the flock of Chrift a fhepherd, not a wolf ; feed them, devour them not. Hold up the weak, heal the fick, bind up the broken, bring again the outcafts, feek the loft. Be fo merciful, that you be not too remifs ; fo minifter difcipline that you forget not mercy ; that when the Chief Shepherd fhall appear, you may receive the never-fading crown of glory, through Jefus Chrift our Lord. *Amen.*

*Then the Superintendant ſhall proceed in the Commu-nion Service , with whom the newly-ordained Super-intendant, and other Perſons preſent, ſhall communi-cate.*

*And for the laſt Collect, immediately before the Bene-diction, ſhall be ſaid theſe Prayers.*

MOST merciful Father, we befeech thee to fend down upon this thy fervant thy heavenly blefling, and fo endue him with thy Holy Spirit, that he, preaching thy word, may not only be ear-neft to reprove, befeech, and rebuke with all pa-tience and doctrine, but alfo may be to fuch as be-lieve a wholefome example in word, in converfa-tion,

tion, in love, in faith, in chaſtity, and in purity; that faithfully fulfilling his courſe, at the latter day he may receive the crown of righteouſneſs laid up by the Lord, the righteous Judge, who liveth and reigneth one God with the Father and the Holy Ghoſt, world without end. *Amen.*

PRevent us, O Lord, in all our doings with thy moſt gracious favour, and further us with thy continual help, that in all our works begun, continued and ended in thee, we may glorify thy holy Name, and finally, by thy mercy, obtain everlaſting life, through Jeſus Chriſt our Lord. *Amen.*

THE peace of God, which paſſeth all underſtanding, keep your hearts and minds in the knowledge and love of God, and of his Son Jeſus Chriſt our Lord; and the bleſſing of God Almighty the Father, the Son, and the Holy Ghoſt, be amongſt you, and remain with you always. *Amen.*

ARTICLES

# ARTICLES of RELIGION.

### I. *Of Faith in the Holy Trinity.*

THERE is but one living and true God, ever-lafting, without body, parts, or paffions; of infinite power, wifdom, and goodnefs; the Maker and Preferver of all things both vifible and invifible. And in unity of this Godhead there are three Per-fons of one fubftance, power, and eternity; the Father, the Son, and the Holy Ghoft.

### II. *Of the Word, or Son of God, who was made very Man.*

THE Son, who is the Word of the Father, be-gotten from everlafting of the Father, the very and eternal God, of one fubftance with the Father, took man's nature in the womb of the bleffed Virgin: fo that two whole and perfect na-tures, that is to fay, the Godhead and Manhood, were joined together in one Perfon, never to be divided, whereof is one Chrift, very God, and very man, who truly fuffered, was crucified, dead, and buried, to reconcile his Father to us, and to be a facrifice, not only for original guilt, but alfo for actual fins of men.

III. *Of*

### III. Of the Resurrection of Christ.

CHRIST did truly rise again from the dead, and took again his body, with all things appertaining to the Perfection of Man's Nature, wherewith he ascended into Heaven, and there sitteth until he return to judge all men at the last day.

### IV. Of the Holy Ghost.

THE Holy Ghost, proceeding from the Father and the Son, is of one Substance, Majesty, and Glory, with the Father and the Son, very and eternal God.

### V. Of the Sufficiency of the Holy Scriptures for Salvation.

HOLY Scripture containeth all things necessary to Salvation : so that whatsoever is not read therein, or may be proved thereby, is not to be required of any man, that it should be believed as an Article of the Faith, or be thought requisite or necessary to salvation. In the name of the Holy Scripture we do understand those Canonical Books of the Old and New Testament, of whose authority was never any doubt in the Church.

### Of the Names of the Canonical Books.

GEnesis,
  Exodus,
Leviticus,
Numbers,
Deuteronomy,
Joshua,
Judges,
Ruth,
The First Book of Samuel,
The Second Book of Samuel,

The

The Firſt Book of Kings,
The Second Book of Kings,
The Firſt Book of Chronicles,
The Second Book of Chronicles,
The Book of Ezra,
The Book of Nehemiah,
The Book of Heſter,
The Book of Job,
The Pſalms,
The Proverbs,
Eccleſiaſtes, or Preacher,
Cantica, or Songs of Solomon,
Four Prophets the greater,
Twelve Prophets the leſs.

All the Books of the New Teſtament, as they are commonly received, we do receive and account Canonical.

### Of the Old Teſtament.

THE Old Teſtament is not contrary to the New; for both in the Old and New Teſtament ever-laſting life is offered to mankind by Chriſt, who is the only Mediator between God and Man, being both God and Man. Wherefore they are not to be heard, who feign that the old Fathers did look only for tranſitory promiſes Although the law given from God by Moſes, as touching Ceremo-nies and Rites, doth not bind Chriſtians, nor ought the Civil Precepts thereof of neceſſity to be received in any Commonwealth: yet notwith-ſtanding, no Chriſtian whatſoever is free from the obedience of the commandments which are called Moral.

VII. *Of*

### VII. *Of Original or Birth-sin.*

ORiginal Sin standeth not in the following of Adam (as the Pelagians do vainly talk), but it is the corruption of the nature of every man, that naturally is ingendered of the offspring of Adam, whereby man is very far gone from original righteousness, and of his own nature inclined to evil, and that continually.

### VIII. *Of Free-will.*

THE condition of man after the fall of Adam is such that he cannot turn and prepare himself by his own natural stren th and works to faith, and calling upon God: Wherefore we have no power to do good works pleasant and acceptable to God, without the grace of God by Christ preventing us, that we may have a good-will, and working with us, when we have that good-will.

### IX. *Of the Justification of Man.*

WE are accounted righteous before God, only for the merit of our Lord and Saviour Jesus Christ, by faith, and not for our own works or deservings: wherefore, that we are justified by faith only, is a most wholesome doctrine, and very full of comfort.

### X. *Of good Works.*

ALthough good Works, which are the fruits of Faith, and follow after Justification, cannot put away our sins, and endure the severity of God's judgment; yet are they pleasing and acceptable to God in Christ, and spring out of a true and lively Faith, insomuch that by them a lively Faith may be as evidently known, as a tree discerned by its fruit.

XI. *Of*

### XI. *Of Works of Supererogation.*

Oluntary Works, befides, over and above God's Commandments, which they call Works of Supererogation, cannot be taught without arrogancy and impiety. For by them men do declare, That they do not only render unto God as much as they are bound to do, but that they do more for his fake than of bounden duty is required : whereas Chrift faith plainly, When ye have done all that is commanded you, fay, We are unprofitable fervants.

### XII. *Of Sin after Juftification.*

NOT every fin willingly committed after Juftification, is the fin againft the Holy Ghoft, and unpardonable. Wherefore the grant of repentance is not to be denied to fuch as fall into fin, after juftification : after we have received the Holy Ghoft, we may depart from grace given, and fall into fin, and by the grace of God rife again, and amend our lives. And therefore they are to be condemned who fay they can no more fin as long as they live here, or deny the place of forgivenefs to fuch as truly repent.

### XIII. *Of the Church.*

THE vifible Church of Chrift is a Congregation of faithful men, in the which the pure Word of God is preached, and the Sacraments duly adminiftered according to Chrift's Ordinance, in all thofe things that of neceffity are requifite to the fame.

### XIV. *Of Purgatory.*

THE Romifh Doctrine concerning Purgatory, Pardons, Worfhipping, and Adoration, as well of Images, as of Reliques, and alfo Invoca-

tion

tion of Saints, is a fond thing vainly invented, and grounded upon no warrant of Scripture, but repugnant to the Word of God.

### XV. Of speaking in the Congregation in such a Tongue as the People understand.

IT is a thing plainly repugnant to the Word of God, and the Custom of the Primitive Church, to have Publick Prayer in the Church, or to minister the Sacraments in a Tongue not understood by the People.

### XVI. Of the Sacraments.

SAcraments ordained of Christ, are not only badges or tokens of Christian Men's Profession; but rather they are certain Signs of Grace, and God's good Will towards us, by the which he doth work invisibly in us, and doth not only quicken, but also strengthen and confirm our faith in him.

There are two Sacraments ordained of Christ our Lord in the Gospel; that is to say, Baptism, and the Supper of the Lord.

Those five commonly called Sacraments; that is to say, Confirmation, Penance, Orders, Matrimony, and extreme Unction, are not to be counted for Sacraments of the Gospel, being such as have grown, partly of the corrupt following of the Apostles, partly are states of life allowed in the Scriptures: but yet have not the like nature of Baptism and the Lord's Supper, because they have not any visible Sign or Ceremony ordained of God.

The sacraments were not ordained of Christ to be gazed upon, or to be carried about; but that we should duly use them. And in such only as worthily receive the same, they have a wholsome effect or operation: but they that receive them unworthily

thily, purchafe to themfelves condemnation, as Saint *Paul* faith.

## XVII. *Of Baptifm.*

BAptifm is not only a fign of profeffion, and mark of difference, whereby Chriftians are diftinguifhed from others that are not baptized; but it is alfo a fign of regeneration, or the new birth. The baptifm of young children is to be retained in the church.

## XVIII. *Of the Lord's Supper.*

THE Supper of the Lord is not only a fign of the love that Chriftians ought to have among themfelves one to another, but rather is a facrament of our redemption by Chrift's death: Infomuch. that to fuch as rightly, worthily, and with faith receive the fame, the bread which we break is a partaking of the body of Chrift; and likewife the cup of bleffing is a partaking of the blood of Chrift.

Tranfubftantiation, or the change of the fubftance of bread and wine in the fupper of the Lord, cannot be proved by holy writ; but is repugnant to the plain words of Scripture, overthroweth the nature of a facrament, and hath given occafion to many fuperftitions.

The body of Chrift is given, taken, and eaten in the fupper, only after an heavenly and fpiritual manner. And the mean whereby the body of Chrift is received and eaten in the fupper, is faith.

The facrament of the Lord's fupper was not by Chrift's ordinance referved, carried about, lifted up, or worfhipped.

2

## XIX. *Of both Kinds.*

THE cup of the Lord is not to be denied to the lay-people; for both the parts of the Lord's Supper, by Chriſt's ordinance and commandment, ought to be miniſtered to all Chriſtians alike.

## XX. *Of the One Oblation of Chriſt, finiſhed upon the Croſs.*

THE offering of Chriſt once made, is that perfeſt redemption, propitiation, and ſatisfaſtion for all the ſins of the whole world, both original and aſtual ; and there is none other ſatisfaſtion for ſin but that alone. Wheıefore the ſacrifice of maſſes, in the which it is commonly ſaid that the prieſt doth offer Chriſt for the quick and the dead, to have remiſſion of pain or guilt, is a blaſphemous fable, and dangerous decei.

## XXI. *Of the Marriage of Miniſters.*

THE miniſters of Chriſt are not commanded by God's law either to vow the eſtate of ſingle life, or to abſtain from marriage ; therefore it is lawful for them, as for all other Chriſtians, to marry at their own diſcretion, as they ſhall judge the ſame to ſerve beſt to godlineſs.

## XXII. *Of the Rites and Ceremonies of Churches.*

IT is not neceſſary that rites and ceremonies ſhould in all places be the ſame, or exaſtly alike ; for they have been always different, and may be changed according to the diverſity of countries, times, and men's manners, ſo that nothing be ordained againſt God's word. Whoſoever, through his private judgment, willingly and purpoſely doth openly break the rites and ceremonies

O

of

of the church to which he belongs, which are not repugnant to the word of God, and are ordained and approved by common authority, ought to be rebuked openly, that others may fear to do the like, as one that offendeth against the common order of the church, and woundeth the consciences of weak brethren.

Every particular church may ordain, change, or abolish rites and ceremonies, so that all things may be done to edification.

### XXIII.  *Of Christian Men's Goods.*

THE riches and goods of Christians are not common as touching the right, title, and possession of the same, as some do falsely boast. Notwithstanding, every man ought, of such things as he possesseth, liberally to give alms to the poor according to his ability.

### XXIV.  *Of a Christian Man's Oath.*

AS we confess that vain and rash swearing is forbidden Christian men by our Lord Jesus Christ, and *James* his apostle ; so we judge that the Christian religion doth not prohibit, but that a man may swear when the magistrate requireth, in a cause of faith and charity, so it be done according to the Prophet's teaching, in justice, judgment, and truth.

### F I N I S.

brought out of darknefs and error, into the clear
light and true knowledge of thee, and of thy Son
Jefus Chrift.    Therefore with Angels, &c.

### Upon the Feaft of Trinity.

WHO art one God, one Lord ; not one only
perfon, but three perfons in one fubftance.
For that which we believe of the glory of the Fa-
ther, the fame we believe of the Son, and of the
Holy Ghoft, without any difference or inequality.
Therefore with Angels, &c.

*After each of which Prefaces fhall immediately be faid;*

THerefore with Angels and Archangels, and with
all the company of heaven, we laud and magnify thy glorious Name, evermore praifing thee,
and faying, Holy, holy, holy, Lord God of hofts,
heaven and earth are full of thy glory.    Glory be
to thee, O Lord moft high.    Amen.

*Then fhall the Elder, kneeling down at the Table, fay,
in the Name of all them that fhall receive the Communion,   this Prayer following ;   the People alfo
kneeling :*

WE do not prefume to come to this thy Table,
O merciful Lord, trufting in our own righteoufnefs, but in thy manifold and great mercies.
We are not worthy fo much as to gather up the
crumbs under thy table.   But thou art the fame
Lord, whofe property is always to have mercy :
Grant us therefore, gracious Lord, fo to eat the
flefh of thy dear Son Jefus Chrift, and to drink his
blood, that our finful bodies may be made clean by
his body, and our fouls wafhed through his moft
precious blood, and that we may evermore dwell in
him, and he in us. *Amen.*

*Then*

*Then the Elder fhall fay the Prayer of Confecration, as
fol/oweth :*

ALmighty God, our heavenly Father, who, of
thy tender mercy, didft give thine only Son
Jefus Chrift to fuffer death upon the crofs for our
redemption ; who made there (by his oblation
of himfelf once offered) a full, perfect, and fuffi-
cient facrifice, oblation, and fatisfaction for the fins
of the whole world ; and did inftitute, and in his
holy Gofpel command us to continue, a perpetual
memory of that his precious death until his coming again ; hear us, O merciful Father, we moft
humbly befeech thee, and grant that we, receiving
thefe thy creatures of bread and wine, according to
thy Son our Saviour Jefus Chrift's holy inftitution,
in remembrance of his death and paffion, may be
partakers of his moft bleffed Body and Blood :
who, in the fame night that he was betrayed, took
bread ; and when he had given thanks, he brake
it, and gave it to his difciples, faying, Take, eat ;
this is my Body which is given for you : Do this
in remembrance of me. Likewife, after fupper,
he took the cup ; and when he had given thanks,
he gave it to them, faying, Drink ye all of this ;
for this is my blood of the New Teftament, which
is fhed for you, and for many, for the remiffion of
fins : Do this, as oft as ye fhall drink it, in remembrance of me. *Amen.*

*Then fhall the Minifter firft receive the Communion in
both kinds himfelf, and then proceed to deliver the
fame to the other Minifters in like manner, (if any
be prefent) and after that to the People alfo, in
order, into their Hands. And when he delivereth
the Bread to any one, he fhall fay,*

THE Body of our Lord Jefus Chrift, which was
given for thee, preferve thy body and foul unto
everlafting life. Take and eat this in remem-

not enter therein. And he took them up in his arms, put his hands upon them, and bleffed them,

*Then ſholl the Miniſtei ſay,*

ALmighty and everlaſting God, heavenly Father, we give thee humble thanks that thou haſt vouchſafed to call us to the knowledge of thy grace and faith in thee, increaſe this knowledge, and confirm this faith in us evermore. Give thy Holy Spirit to *this Infant,* that *he* may be born again, and be made *an heir* of everlaſting ſalvation, through our Lord Jeſus Chriſt, who liveth and reigneth with thee and the Holy Spirit, now and for ever. *Amen.*

O Merciful God, grant that the old Adam in *this Child* may be ſo buried, that the new man may be raiſed up in *him. Amen.*

Grant that all carnal affeᵭtions may die in *him,* and that all things belonging to the Spirit may live and grow in *him. Amen.*

Grant that *he* may have power and ſtrength to have viᵭtory, and to triumph againſt the devil, the world, and the fleſh. *Amen.*

Grant that whoſoever is dedicated to thee by our office and miniſtry, may alſo be endued with heavenly virtues, and everlaſtingly rewarded, through thy mercy, O bleſſed Lord God, who doſt live and govern all things, world without end. *Amen.*

ALmighty everliving God, whoſe moſt dearly beloved Son Jeſus Chriſt, for the forgiveneſs of our ſins, did ſhed out of his moſt precious ſide both water and blood, and gave commandment to his diſciples that they ſhould go teach all nations, and baptize them in the Name of the Father, and of the Son, and of the Holy Ghoſt, regard, we beſeech

feech thee, the fupplications of thy congregation ; fanctify this water to the myftical wafhing away of fin ; and grant that *this Child*, now to be baptized, may receive the fulnefs of thy grace, and ever remain in the number of thy faithful and elect children, through Jefus Chrift our Lord. *Amen.*

*Then the Minifter fhall take the Child into his Hands, and fay to the Friends of the Child,*
Name this Child.

*And then, naming it after them, he fhall dip it in the Water, or fprinkle it therewith, faying,*

N. I baptize thee, in the Name of the Father, and of the Son, and of the Holy Ghoft. *Amen.*

*Then fhall the Minifter fay,*

SEeing now, dearly beloved brethren, that *this Child is* grafted into the body of Chrift's Church, let us give thanks unto Almighty God for thefe benefits, and with one accord make our prayers unto him, that *this Child* may lead the reft of *his life* according to this beginning.

*Then fhall be faid, all kneeling,*

OUR Father who art in heaven, Hallowed be thy Name ; Thy kingdom come ; Thy will be done on earth, as it is in heaven : Give us this day our daily bread ; And forgive us our trefpaffes, as we forgive them that trefpafs againft us : And lead us not into temptation ; But deliver us from evil. *Amen.*

*Then fhall the Minifter fay,*

WE yield thee hearty thanks, moft merciful Father, that it hath pleafed thee to receive *this Infant* for thine own *Child* by adoption, and to incorporate *him* into thy holy Church. And humbly

bly we befeech thee to grant, that *he*, being dead unto fin, and living unto righteoufnefs, and being buried with Chrift in his death, may crucify the old man, and utterly abolifh the whole body of fin; and that, as *he is* made *partaker* of the death of thy Son, *he* may alfo be *partaker* of his refurrection; fo that finally, with the refidue of thy holy Church, *he* may be *an inheritor* of thine everlafting kingdom, through Chrift our Lord. *Amen.*

---

## The Miniftration of Baptism to fuch as are of Riper Years.

### *The Minifter fhall fay,*

DEarly beloved, forafmuch as all men are conceived and born in fin (and that which is born of the flefh is flefh, and they that are in the flefh cannot pleafe God, but live in fin, committing many actual tranfgreffions); and that our Saviour Chrift faith, None can enter into the kingdom of God, except he be regenerate and born anew of water and of the Holy Ghoft; I befeech you to call upon God the Father, through our Lord Jefus Chrift, that of his bounteous goodnefs he will grant to *thefe Perfons*, that which by nature *they* cannot have; that *they* may be baptized with Water and the Holy Ghoft, and received into Chrift's holy Church, and be made lively *members* of the fame.

### *Then fhall the Minifter fay,*

Let us pray..

*( And here all the Congregation fhall kneel.)*

ALmighty and everlafting God, who of thy great mercy didft fave Noah and his family in the ark from perifhing by water; and alfo didft

**fafely**

fafely lead the children of Ifrael thy people through the Red Sea, figuring thereby thy holy Baptifm ; and by the Baptifm of thy well-beloved Son Jefus Chrift in the river Jordan, didft fanctify the element of water to the myftical wafhing away of fin ; We befeech thee, for thine infinite mercies, that thou wilt mercifully look upon *thefe* thy *Servants* ; wafh *them* and fanctify *them* with the Holy Ghoft ; that *they* being delivered from thy wrath, may be received into the ark of Chrift's Church ; and being ftedfaft in faith, joyful through hope, and rooted in charity, may fo pafs the waves of this troublefome world, that finally *they* may come to the land of everlafting life ; there to reign with thee, world without end, through Jefus Chrift our Lord. *Amen.*

A Lmighty and immortal God, the aid of all that need, the helper of all that flee to thee for fuccour, the life of them that believe, and the refurrection of the dead ; We call upon thee for *thefe Perfons* ; that *they* coming to thy holy Baptifm, may receive remiffion of *their* fins by fpiritual regeneration. Receive *them*, O Lord, as thou haft promifed by thy well-beloved Son, faying, Afk, and ye fhall receive ; feek, and ye fhall find ; knock, and it fhall be opened unto you : So give now unto us that afk ; let us that feek find ; open the gate unto us that knock ; that *thefe Perfons* may enjoy the everlafting benediction of thy heavenly wafhing, and may come to the eternal kingdom which thou haft promifed by Chrift our Lord. *Amen.*

*Then*

# A
# COLLECTION
# OF
# PSALMS and HYMNS

## PSALM 1

1. Blest is the man, and none but he,
    Who walks not with ungodly men,
    Nor stands their evil deeds to see,
    Nor fits the innocent t'arraign,
    The persecutor's guilt to share,
    Oppressive in the scorner's chair.

2. Obedience is his pure delight,
    To do the pleasure of his Lord;
    His exercise by day and night
    To search his soul-converting word,
    The law of liberty to prove,
    The perfect law of life and love.

3. Fast by the streams of paradise
    He as a pleasant plant shall grow:
    The tree of righteousness shall rise,
    And all his blooming honours shew,
    Spread out his boughs, and flourish fair,
    And fruit unto perfection bear.

4. His verdant leaf shall never fade,
    His works of faith shall never cease,
    His happy toil shall all succeed
    Whom God himself delights to bless:
    But no success th' ungodly find,
    Scatter'd like chaff before the wind.

5. No portion and no place have they
    With those whom God vouchsafes t'approve:
    Cast in the dreadful judgment-day,
    Who trample on their Saviour's love;
    Who here their bleeding Lord deny,
    Shall perish, and for ever die.

## PSALM III

1. See, O Lord, my foes increase,
    Mark the troublers of my peace,
    Fiercely 'gainst my soul they rise,
    "Heaven," they say, "Its help denies,
    "Help he seeks from God in vain,
    "God hath given him up to man."

2. But thou art a shield for me,
    Succor still I find in thee;
    Now thou liftest up my head,
    Now I glory in thine aid;
    Confident in thy defence,
    Strong in thine omnipotence.

3. To the Lord I cried, the cry
    Brought my helper from the sky;
    By my kind protector kept,
    Safe I laid me down and slept,
    Slept within his arms and rose;
    Blest him for the calm repose.

4. Kept by him, I cannot fear
    Sin, the world, or Satan near,
    All their hosts my soul defies:
    Lord, in my behalf arise,
    Save me, for in faith I call,
    Save me, O my God from all.

5. Thou hast sav'd me heretofore,
    Thou hast quell'd the adverse power,
    Pluck'd me from the jaws of death,
    Broke the roaring lion's teeth;
    Still from all my foes defend,
    Save me, save me to the end.

6. Thine it is, O Lord, to save;
    Strength in thee thy people have:
    Safe from sin in thee they rest,
    With the gospel-blessing blest,
    Wait to see the perfect grace,
    Heaven on earth in Jesu's face.

## PSALM IV

1. God of my righteousness,
   Thy humble suppliant hear,
Thou hast reliev'd me in distress,
   And thou art always near.
   Again thy mercy shew,
   The peaceful answer send,
Assuage my grief, relieve my woe,
   And all my troubles end.

2. How long ye sons of men,
   Will ye blaspheme aloud,
My honour wrong, my glory stain,
   And vilify my God?
   How long will ye delight
   In vanity and vice
Madly against the righteous fight,
   And follow after lies!

3. Know, for himself, the Lord
   Hath surely set apart
The man that trembles at his word,
   The man of upright heart:
   And when to him I pray,
   He promises to hear,
And help me in my evil day,
   And answer all my prayer.

4. Ye sinners, stand in awe,
   And from your sins depart,
Out of the evil world withdraw,
   And commune with your heart:
   In thinking of his love
   Be day and night employ'd,
Be still; nor in his presence move,
   But wait upon your God.

5. Offer your prayer and praise,
   Which he will not despise,
Through *Jesus Christ* your righteousness,
   Accepted sacrifice.
   Offer your heart's desires;
   But trust him alone,
Who gives whatever he requires,
   And freely saves his own.

6. The world with fruitless pain
   Seek happiness below,
What man (they ask, but all in vain)
   The long-fought good will shew?
   The brightness of thy face,
   Give us, O Lord, to see,
Glory on earth begun in grace,
   And happiness in thee.

7. Thou hast on me bestow'd,
   All-gracious as thou art,
The taste divine, the sovereign good,
   And fixt it in my heart:
   Above all earthly bliss
   The sense of sin forgiven,
The hidden joy, the mystic peace,
   The antepast of heaven.

8. The gospel-peace possest,
   Secure in thy defence,
Now, Lord, within thine arms I rest,
   And who shall pluck me thence?
   Nor sin, nor earth, nor hell
   Shall ever more remove,
When all renew'd in thee I dwell,
   And perfected in love.

## PSALM V

1. O Lord, incline thy gracious ear,
      My plaintive sorrows weigh,
   To thee for succour I draw near,
      To thee I humbly pray.
   Still will I call with lifted eyes,
      Come, O my God and king,
   'Till thou regard my ceaseless cries,
      And full deliv'rance bring.

2. On thee, O God of purity,
      I wait for hallowing grace;
   None without holiness shall see
      The glories of thy face:
   In souls unholy and unclean
      Thou never canst delight;
   Nor shall they, while unsav'd from sin,
      Appear before thy sight.

3. Thou hatest all that evil do,
      Or speak iniquity;
   The hearts unkind, and hearts untrue
      Are both abhor'd by thee.
   The greatest and minutest fault
      Shall find its fearful doom,
   Sinners in deed, or word, or thought,
      Thou surely shalt consume.

4. But as for me, with humble fear
      I will approach thy gate,
   Tho' most unworthy to draw near,
      Or in thy courts to wait:
   I trust in thy unbounded grace
      To all so freely given,
   And worship tow'rd thy holy place,
      And lift my soul to heaven.

5. Lead me in all thy righteous ways,
   Nor suffer me to slide,
   Point out the path before my face;
   My God, be thou my guide:
   The cruel power, the guileful art
   Of all my foes suppress,
   Whose throat an open grave, whose heart
   Is desp'rate wickedness.

6. Thou, Lord, shall drive them from thy face,
   And finally consume,
   Thy wrath on the rebellious race
   Shall to the utmost come.
   But all who put their trust in Thee
   Thy mercy shall proclaim,
   And sing with cheerful melody
   Their dear Redeemer's name.

7. Protected by thy guardian grace,
   They shall extol their power,
   Rejoice, give thanks, and shout thy praise,
   And triumph evermore.
   They never shall to evil yield
   Defended from above,
   And kept and cover'd with the shield
   Of thine almighty love.

### PSALM VI

1. Lord, in thy wrath no more chastise,
   Nor let thy whole displeasure rise
   Against a child of man;
   Have mercy, Lord, for I am weak,
   And heal my soul diseas'd and sick,
   And full of sin and pain.

2. Body and soul thy judgments feel,
   Thy heavy wrath afflicts me still;
   O when shall it be o'er!
   Turn thee, O Lord, and save my soul,
   And for thy mercy's sake make whole,
   And bid me sin no more.

3. Here, only here thy love must save,
   I cannot thank thee in the grave,
   Or tell thy pard'ning grace:
   Who dies unpurg'd, for ever dies,
   The sinner, as he falls, he lies
   Shut up in his own place.

4. But shall I to my foes give place?
   Or, in the name of Jesus, chase
   My troubles all away?
   In Jesu's name, I say, depart
   Devils and sins; nor vex my heart,
   For God hath heard me pray.

5. The Lord hath heard my groans and tears,
   The Lord shall still accept my prayers,
   And all my foes o'erthrow;
   Shall conquer and destroy them too,
   And make ev'n me a creature new,
   A sinless saint below.

### PSALM XIII

1. How long wilt Thou forgive me, Lord?
   Wilt Thou for ever hide thy face?
   Leave me unchang'd and unrestor'd,
   An alien from the life of grace?

2. Hear me, O Lord, my God, and weigh
   My sorrows in the scale of love,
   Lighten mine eyes, restore the day.
   The darkness from my soul remove.

3. Thou wilt, thou wilt! my hope returns:
   A sudden spirit of faith I feel,
   My heart in fervent wishes burns,
   And God shall there for ever dwell.

4. My trust is in thy gracious power,
   I glory in salvation near,
   Rejoice in hope of that glad hour,
   When perfect love shall cast out fear.

5. I sing the goodness of the Lord,
   The goodness I experience now,
   And still I hang upon thy word,
   My Saviour to the utmost thou.

6. Thy love I ever shall proclaim,
   A monument of thy mercy I,
   And praise the mighty Jesu's name,
   Jesus the Lord, the Lord most high.

### PSALM XXXVIII

1. Amidst thy wrath remember love,
   Restore thy servant, Lord!
   Nor let a father's chastening prove
   Like an avenger's sword!

2. My sins a heavy burden are,
   And o'er my head are gone;
   Too heavy they for me to bear,
   Too great for me t'atone.

3. My thoughts are like a troubled sea,
   My head still bending down:
   And I go mourning all the day,
   Father, beneath thy frown.

C-3

4. All my desire to Thee is known,
   Thine eyes count every tear;
   And every sigh, and every groan,
   Is noticed by thine ear.

5. Thou art my God, my only hope,
   O hearken to my cry:
   O bear my fainting spirits up,
   When Satan bids me die.

6. Lord, I confess my guilt to thee,
   I grieve for all my sin;
   My helpless impotence I see,
   And beg support divine.

7. O God, forgive my follies past;
   Be Thou for ever nigh!
   O Lord of my salvation, haste,
   And save me, or I die!

PSALM LI

1. O thou that hear'st when sinners cry,
   Tho' all my crimes before Thee lie,
   Behold me not with angry look,
   But blot their mem'ry from thy book.

2. Create my nature pure within,
   And form my soul averse from sin
   Let thy good spirit ne'er depart,
   Nor hide thy presence from my heart.

3. I cannot live without thy light,
   Cast out and banish'd from thy sight:
   Thy saving strength, O Lord, restore,
   And guard me that I fall no more.

4. Tho' I have griev'd thy Spirit, Lord,
   His help and comfort still afford;
   And let a wretch come near thy throne
   To plead the merits of thy Son.

5. My soul lies humbled in the dust,
   And owns thy dreadful sentence just.
   Look down, O Lord, with pitying eye,
   And save the soul condemned to die.

6. Then will I Teach the world thy ways;
   Sinners shall learn thy sovereign grace;
   I'll lead them to my Saviour's blood,
   And they shall praise a pard'ning God.

7. O may thy Love inspire my tongue,
   Salvation shall be all my song;
   And all my powers shall join to bless
   The Lord, my strength and righteousness.

*The same*
*Part the First.*

1. God of unfathomable love,
   Whose bowels of compassion move
   Tow'rds *Adam's* helpless race,
   See, at thy feet, a sinner see,
   In tender mercy look on me,
   And all my sins efface.

2. O let thy love to me o'erflow
   Thy multitude of mercies shew,
   Abundantly forgive:
   Remove th' unsufferable load,
   Blot out my sins with sacred blood,
   And bid the sinner live.

3. Take all the power of sin away,
   Nor let in me its being stay,
   My inmost soul convert:
   Wash me from all my filth of sin,
   Come, Lord, and make me throughly clean,
   Create me pure in heart.

4. For O my sins I now confess,,
   Bewail my desp'rate wickedness,
   And sue to be forgiven,
   I have abus'd thy patient grace,
   I have provok'd Thee to thy face,
   And dar'd the wrath of heaven.

5. Cast in the mould of sin I am,
   Corrupt throughout my ruin'd frame,
   My essence all unclean;
   My total fall from God I mourn,
   In sin I was conceiv'd and born,
   Whate'er I am is sin.

6. But Thou requirest all our hearts,
   Truth rooted in the inward parts,
   Unspotted purity;
   And by thy grace I humbly trust,
   To learn the wisdom of the Just,
   In secret taught by Thee.

*Part the Second.*

1. Surely Thou wilt the grace impart
   Sprinkle the blood upon my heart
   Which did for sinners flow,
   The blood that purges every sin,
   The blood that soon shall wash me clean,
   And make me white as snow.

2. Thou wilt the mournful spirit cheer,
   And grant me once again to hear
      Thy sweet forgiving voice,
   That all my bones and inmost soul,
   Broken by Thee, By Thee made whole,
      May in thy strength rejoice.

3. From my misdeeds avert thy face,
   The strength of sin by pardn'ing grace,
      Of all my sin remove;
   Forgive, O Lord, but change me too,
   But perfectly my soul renew
      By sanctifying love.

4. My wretchedness to Thee convert,
   Give me an humble contrite heart,
      My fallen soul restore:
   Let me the life divine attain,
   The image of my God regain,
      And never lose it more.

### Part the Third.

1. Have patience, till by Thee renew'd
   I live the sinless life of God,
      Here let thy spirit stay:
   Tho' I have griev'd the gentle Dove,
   Ah! do not quite withdraw thy love,
      Or take thy grace away.

2. The comfort of thy help restore,
   Assist me now as heretofore,
      O lift thou up my head,
   The spirit of thy power impart,
   Stablish and keep my faithful heart,
      And make me free indeed.

3. Then shall I teach the world thy ways,
   Thy mercy mild and pard'ning grace
      For every sinner free,
   Till sinners to thy grace submit,
   And fall at their Redeemer's feet,
      And weep, and love like me.

4. O might I weep, and love Thee now,
   God of my health, my Saviour Thou,
      Thou only canst release
   My soul from all iniquity;
   O speak the word, and set me free,
      And bid me go in peace.

5. So shall I sing the Saviour's name,
   The gift of righteousness proclaim,
      Thine all-redeeming grace:
   Open my lips, almighty Lord,
   That I thy mercy may record,
      And glory in thy praise.

### Part the Fourth.

1. No creature-good dost thou desire,
   No costly sacrifice require;
      Thy pleasure is to give:
   Thou only seekest me, not mine,
   Thou wouldst that I should take of Thine,
      Should all thy grace receive.

2. A wounded spirit, by sin distrest,
   A broken heart that pants for rest,
      This is the sacrifice
   Well-pleasing in the sight of God;
   A sinner crush'd beneath his load
   Thou never wilt despise.

3. Then hear the contrite sinner's prayer,
   And every ruin'd soul repair,
      Remember *Sion's* woe;
   Shew forth thy sanctifying grace,
   And for thyself vouchsafe to raise
      A glorious church below.

4. When Thou hast seal'd thy people's peace,
   Their sacrifice of righteousness,
      Their gifts Thou wilt approve,
   Their every thought, and word, and deed,
   That from a living faith proceed,
      And all are wrought in love.

5. Laid on the altar of thy Son,
   Pleasing to Thee thro' Christ alone,
      Their dear peculiar race
   Their grateful sacrifice shall bring,
   And hymn their Father and their King
      In ending songs of praise.

### PSALM LXIII

1. Great God, indulge my humble claim;
      Be thou my hope, my joy, my rest!
   The glories that compose thy name,
      Stands all engag'd to make me blest.

2. Thou great and good, thou just and wise,
      Thou art my Father and my God!
   And I am thine by sacred ties,
      Thy son, thy servant bought with blood.

3. With heart and eyes and lifted hands,
      For Thee I long, to Thee I look;
   As travellers in thirsty lands
      Pant for the cooling water-brook.

4. Even life itself, without thy love,
No lasting pleasure can afford;
Yea, 'twould a tiresome burden prove,
If I were banish'd from Thee, Lord!

5. I'll lift my hands, I'll raise my voice,
While I have breath to pray or praise,
This Work shall make my heart rejoice,
And spend the remnant of my days.

## PSALM LXXX
### Part the First.

1. Shepherd of souls, the great, the good,
Who leadest *Israel* like a sheep,
Present to guard, and give them food,
And kindly in the bosom keep;

2. Hear thy afflicted people's prayer,
Arise out of thy holy place,
Stir up thy strength, thine arm make bare,
And vindicate thy chosen race.

3. Haste to our help, thou God of love,
Supreme almighty King of kings,
Descend all-glorious from above,
Come flying on the Cherubs' wings.

4. Turn us again, O Lord, and shew
The brightness of thy lovely face,
So that we all be saints below,
And sav'd and perfected in grace.

### Part the Second.

1. Turn thee again, O Lord our God,
Look down with pity from above,
O lay aside thy vengeful rod,
And visit us in pard'ning love:

2. So will we not from thee go back,
If thou our fallen souls restore:
No, never more will we forsake,
No, never will we grieve thee more.

3. Revive, O god of power, revive
Thy work in our degen'rate days,
O let us by thy mercy live,
And all our lives shall speak thy praise.

4. Turn us again, O Lord, and shew
The brightness of thy lovely face,
So shall we all be saints below,
And sav'd and perfected in grace.

## PSALM XC

1. O God, our help in ages past,
Our hope for years to come,
Our shelter from the stormy blast,
And our eternal home.

2. Under the shadow of thy throne,
Still may we dwell secure:
Sufficient is thy arm alone,
And our defence is sure.

3. Before the hills in order stood,
Or earth receiv'd her frame,
From everlasting thou art God,
To endless years the same.

4. A thousand ages in thy sight
Are like an evening gone,
Short as the watch that ends the night
Before the rising sun.

5. The busy tribes of flesh and blood,
With all their cares and fears,
Are carried downward with the flood,
And lost in following years.

6. Time, like an ever-rolling stream,
Bears all its sons away;
They fly forgotten, as a dream
Dies at the opening day.

7. O God, our help in ages past,
Our hope for years to come,
Be Thou our guard while life shall last,
And our perpetual home.

## PSALM XCI

1. He that hath God his guardian made,
Shall under the Almighty's shade
Secure and undisturb'd abide:
Thus to my soul of him I'll say;
He is my fortress and my stay,
My God, in whom I will confide.

2. Thy tender love and watchful care
Shall free me from the fowler's snare,
And from the noisome pestilence:
Thou over me thy wings shalt spread,
And cover my unguarded head;
Thy truth shall be my strong defence.

3. No terrors that surprise by night,
    Shall thy undaunted courage fright;
        No deadly shafts that fly by day:
    Nor plague of unknown rise that kills
    In darkness, nor infectious ills
        That in the hottest seasons slay.

4. A thousand at thy side shall die,
    At thy right-hand ten thousand lie,
        While thy firm health untouch'd remains:
    Thou only shalt look on and see
    The wicked's dismal tragedy,
        And count the sinner's mournful gains.

5. Because with well-plac'd confidence
    Thou mak'st the Lord thy sure defence,
        And on the highest dost rely;
    Therefore no ill shall thee befall,
    Nor to thy healthful dwelling shall
        Any infectious plague draw nigh.

6. For he throughout thy happy days,
    To keep thee safe in all thy ways
        Shall give his angels strict commands;
    And they, lest thou shouldst chance to meet
    With some rough stone to wound thy feet,
        Shall bear thee safely in their hands.

### PSALM XCIII

1. With glory clad, with strength array'd,
        The Lord that o'er all nature reigns,
    The world's foundations strongly laid,
        And the vast fabric still sustains.

2. How sure establsh'd is thy throne,
        Which shall no change or period see;
    For thou, O Lord, and thou alone
        Art king from all eternity.

3. The floods, O Lord, lift up their voice,
        And toss the troubled waves on high,
    But God above can still their noise,
        And make the angry sea comply.

4. Thy promise, Lord, is ever sure;
        And they that in thy house would dwell,
    That happy station to secure,
        Must still in holiness excel.

### PSALM CXXI

1. To heaven I lift my waiting eyes,
        There all my hopes are laid:
    The Lord that built the earth and skies
        Is my perpetual aid.

2. Their feet, O Lord, shall never fall,
        Whom thou vouchsaf'st to keep:
    Thy ear attends the softest call.
        Thy eyes can never sleep,

3. Thou wilt sustain our feeble powers
        With thy almighty arm:
    Thou watchest our unguarded hours
        Against invading harm.

4. Nor scorching sun nor sickly moon,
        Shall have thy leave to smite;
    Thou shield'st our heads from burning noon;
        From blasting damps at night.

5. He guards our souls, he keeps our breath,
        Where thickest dangers come;
    Go and return secure from death,
        'Till God commands thee home.

### PSALM CXXX

1. Out of the depth of *self-despair*
        To Thee, O Lord, I cry;
    My misery mark, attend my prayer,
        And bring salvation nigh.

2. Death's sentence in myself I feel,
        Beneath thy wrath I faint;
    O let thine ear consider well
        The voice of my complaint.

3. If thou art rig'rously severe,
        Who may the test abide?
    Where shall the man of sin appear,
        Or how be justified?

But O! forgiveness is with thee,
        That sinners may adore,
With filial fear thy goodness see,
        And  never grieve thee more.

4. I look to see his lovely face,
        I wait to meet my Lord;
    My longing soul expects his grace,
        An rests upon his word.

5. My soul, while still to him it flies,
        Prevents the morning-ray;
    O that his mercy's beams would rise,
        And bring the gospel-day!

6. Ye faithful souls, confide in God,
        Mercy with him remains,
    Plenteous redemption in his blood,
        To  wash out all your stains.

7. His *Israel* himself shall clear,
   From all their sins redeem;
   The Lord our righteousness is near,
   And we are just in him.

### PSALM CXXXIX
*Part the First*

1. Lord, all I am is known to thee,
   In vain my soul would try
   To shun thy presence, or to flee
   The notice of thine eye.

2. Thy all-surrounding sight surveys
   my rising and my rest,
   My public walks, my private ways,
   The secrets of my breast.

3. My thoughts lie open to thee, Lord,
   Before they're form'd within;
   And ere my lips pronounce the word,
   Thou know'st the sense I mean.

4. O wondrous knowledge, deep and high,
   Where can a creature hide?
   Within thy circling arms I lie
   Beset on every side.

5. So let thy grace surround me still,
   And like a bulwark prove,
   To guard my soul from ev'ry ill,
   Secur'd by sov'reign love.

*Part the Second.*

1. Lord, where shall guilty souls retire
   Forgotten and unknown?
   In hell they meet thy vengeful ire,
   In heav'n thy glorious throne.

2. Should I suppress my vital breath,
   T' escape the wrath divine,
   Thy voice would break the bars of death,
   And make the grave resign.

3. If wing'd with beams of morning-light
   I fly beyond the west,
   Thy hand, which must support my flight,
   Would soon betray my rest.

4. If o'er my sins I seek to draw
   The curtains of the night,
   Those flaming eyes that guard thy law
   Would turn the shades to light.

5. The beams of noon, the midnight hour,
   Are both alike to thee:
   O may I ne'er provoke that power
   From which I cannot flee.

*Part the Third.*

1. When I with pleasing wonder stand,
   And all my frame survey,
   Lord, 'tis thy work; I own thy hand,
   That built my humble clay.

2. Thy hand my heart and reins possess'd,
   Where unborn nature grew,
   Thy wisdom all my features trac'd,
   And all my members drew.

3. Thine eye with tender care, survey'd
   The growth of every part,
   'Till the whole scheme thy thoughts had laid
   Was copy'd by thy art.

4. Heav'n, earth, and sea, and fire, and wind,
   Shew me thy wond'rous skill;
   But I review myself, and find
   Diviner wonders still.

5. Thy awful glories round me shine,
   My flesh proclaims thy praise:
   Lord, to thy works of nature join
   Thy miracles of grace!

*The Creator and Creatures*

1. God is a name my soul adores,
   Th' almighty Three, th' eternal One!
   Nature and grace with all their powers
   Confess the infinite unknown.

2. Thy voice produc'd the sea and spheres,
   Bid the waves roar, and planets shine;
   But nothing like thyself appears
   Thro' all these spacious works of thine.

3. Still restless nature dies and grows,
   From change to change the creatures run;
   Thy being no succession knows,
   And all thy vast designs are one.

4. A glance of thine runs through the globes,
   Rules the bright worlds, and moves their frame;
   Broad sheets of light compose thy robes,
   Thy guards are form'd of living flame.

5. How shall affrighted mortals dare
   To sing thy glory or thy grace?
   Beneath thy feet we lie so far,
   And see but shadows of thy face.

6. Who can behold the blazing light?
   Who can approach consuming flame?
   None but thy wisdom knows thy might,
   None but thy word can speak thy Name.

### Life and Eternity

1. Thee we adore, eternal Name,
   And humbly own to thee
   How feeble is our mortal frame,
   What dying worms we be.

2. Our wasting lives grow shorter still,
   As months and days increase;
   And every beating pulse we tell,
   Leaves but the number less.

3. The year rolls round, and steals away
   The breath that first it gave;
   Whate'er we do, where'er we be,
   We're trav'lling to the grave.

4. Dangers stand thick thro' all the ground
   To push us to the tomb,
   And fierce diseases wait around
   To hurry mortals home.

5. Great God! on what a slender thread
   Hang everlasting things!
   Th' eternal states of all the dead
   Upon life's feeble strings.

6. Infinite joy, and endless woe,
   Attend on every breath;
   And yet how unconcern'd we go
   Upon the brink of death.

7. Waken, O Lord, our drowsy sense,
   To walk this dang'rous road:
   And if our souls are hurried hence,
   May they be found with God.

### Judgement

1. When rising from the bed of death,
   O'erwhelm'd with guilt and fear,
   I view my Maker face to face,
   O how shall I appear!

2. If yet, while pardon may be found,
   And mercy may be sought,
   My soul with inward horror shrinks,
   And trembles at the thought:

3. When thou, O Lord, shalt stand disclos'd
   In majesty severe,
   And sit in judgement on my soul,
   O how shall I appear?

4. O may my broken contrite heart
   Timely my sins lament,
   And early with repentant tears
   Eternal woe prevent.

5. Behold the sorrows of my heart,
   Ere yet it be too late,
   And hear my Saviour's dying groans
   To give those sorrows weight.

6. For never shall my soul despair
   Her pardon to secure;
   Who knows thy only Son as died
   To make that pardon sure.

### On the Crucifixion.

1. From whence these dire portents around,
   That heaven and earth amaze?
   Wherefore do earthquakes cleave the ground,
   Why hides the sun his rays?

2. Not thus did *Sinai's* trembling head
   With sacred horror nod,
   Beneath the dark pavilion spread
   Of legislative God.

3. Thou earth, thy lowest centre shake,
   With Jesu sympathize!
   Thou sun, as hell's deep gloom be black,
   'Tis thy Creator dies.

4. See, streaming from th' accursed tree,
   His all-atoning blood!
   Is this the infinite? 'Tis he,
   My Saviour and my God.

5. For me these pangs his soul assail,
   For me the death is borne;
   My sins gave sharpness to the nail,
   And pointed every thorn.

6. Let sin no more my soul enslave;
   Break, Lord, the tyrant's chain:
   O save me whom thou cam'st to save,
   Nor bleed nor die in vain.

### Sovereignty and Grace.

1. The Lord! how fearful is his name!
   How wide is his command!
   Nature with all her moving frame
   Rests on his mighty hand.

2. Immortal glory forms his throne,
   And light his awful robe,
   While with a smile, or with a frown,
   He manages the globe.

3. A word of his almighty breath
   Can swell or sink the seas,
   Build the vast empires of the earth,
   Or break them as he please.

4. Adoring angels round him fall
   In all their shining forms;
His sov'reign eye looks thro' them all,
   And pities mortal worms.

5. His bowels to our worthless race
   In sweet compassion move;
He clothes his looks with softest grace,
   And takes his title, Love.

6. Now let the Lord for ever reign,
   And sway us as he will;
Sick or in health, in ease or pain,
   We are his children still.

7. No man shall peevish passions rise,
   Our tongues no more complain:
'Tis sov'reign love that lends our joys,
   And love resumes again.

*A Thought in Affliction.*

1. Wilt thou, O Lord, regard my tears,
   The fruit of guilt and fear?
Me, who thy justice hath provok'd,
   O! will thy mercy spare?

2. Yes, for the broken contrite heart,
   Saviour, thy suff'rings plead;
O quench not then the smoking flax,
   Nor break the bruised reed.

3. Thy poor, unworthy servant view,
   Resign'd to thy decree;
Ordain me, or to live or die,
   But live or die in Thee!

4. Upon thy gracious promise, Lord,
   My humbled soul is cast;
O bear me safe, thro' life, thro' death,
   And raise me up at last!

5. Low as this mortal frame must lie,
   This mortal frame shall sing,
Where is thy victory, O grave!
   And where, O death, thy sting!

*The Christian Race.*

1. Awake, our souls, (away our fears,
   Let every trembling thought be gone,)
Awake, and run the heavenly race,
   And put a cheerful courage on.

2. True, 'tis a strait and thorny road,
   And mortal spirits tire and faint:
But we forget the mighty God,
   That feeds the strength of every saint.

3. O mighty God, thy matchless power
   Is ever new, and ever young,
And firm endures while endless years
   Their everlasting circles run.

4. From Thee, the overflowing spring,
   Our souls shall drink a fresh supply;
While such as trust their native strength,
   Shall melt away, and droop and die.

5. Swift as an eagle cuts the air,
   We'll mount aloft to thine abode;
On wings of love our souls shall fly,
   Nor tire amidst the heavenly road.

*The New Creation.*

1. Attend, while God's eternal Son
   Doth his own glories shew:
"Behold, I sit upon my throne
   "Creating all things new.

2. "Nature and sin are past away,
   "And the old *Adam* dies;
"My hands a new foundation lay:
   "See a new world arise!"

3. Mighty Redeemer, set me free
   From my state of sin;
O make my soul alive to thee,
   Create new powers within.

4. Renew my eyes and form my ears,
   And mould my heart afresh;
Give me new passions, joys, and fears,
   And turn the stone to flesh.

5. Far from the regions of the dead,
   From sin, and earth, and hell,
In the new world thy grace hath made,
   May I for ever dwell.

*Christ's Humiliation and Exaltation.*

1. What equal honours shall we bring
   To thee, O Lord, our God the Lamb?
Since all the notes that angels sing
   Are far inferior to thy name.

2. Worthy is he that once was slain,
   That Prince of Peace that groan'd and died;
Worthy to rise, and live, and reign
   At his almighty Father's side.

3. Pride and dominion are his due,
   Who stood condemn'd at *Pilate's* bar;
   Wisdom belongs to Jesus too,
   Tho' he was charg'd with madness here.

4. Honour immortal must be paid
   Instead of scandal and of scorn;
   While glory shines around his head,
   And a bright crown without a thorn.

5. Blessings for ever on the Lamb,
   Who bore our sin, and curse, and pain:
   Let angels found his sacred name,
   And every creature say, *Amen!*

*Waiting for the Spirit of Adoption.*

1. All glory to the dying Lamb,
   And never-ceasing praise,
   While angels live to know thy name,
   Or men to feel thy grace.

2. With this cold stony heart of mine,
   Jesus, to thee I flee:
   And to thy grace my soul resign,
   To be renew'd by Thee.

3. Give me to hide my blushing face,
   While thy dear cross appears;
   Dissolve my heart in thankfulness,
   And melt my eyes to tears.

4. O may the uncorrupted feed
   Abide and reign within,
   And thy life-giving word forbid
   My new-born soul to sin.

5. Father, I wait before thy throne
   Call me a child of thine;
   Send down the spirit of thy Son
   To form my heart divine.

6. There shed thy promis'd love abroad,
   And make my comfort strong;
   Then shall I say, "my father, God!"
   With an unwav'ring tongue.

*Hymn to the Holy Ghost.*

1. Come, Holy Spirit, send down those beams
   Which gently flow in silent streams
      From the eternal throne above:
   Come, thou enricher of the poor,
   Thou bounteous source of all our store,
      Fill us with faith, with hope, and love.

2. Come, thou our soul's delightful guest,
   The wearied pilgrim's sweetest rest,
      The fainting suff'rer's best relief;
   Come, thou our passions cool allay;
   Thy comfort wipes all tears away,
      And turns to peace and joy all grief.

3. Lord, wash our sinful stains away,
   Water from heaven our barren clay,
      Our sickness cure, our bruises heal:
   To thy sweet yoke our stiff necks bow,
   Warm with thy fire our hearts of snow,
      And there enthron'd for ever dwell.

4. All glory to the Sacred Three,
   One everlasting Deity;
      All love and power, and might and praise!
   As at the first, ere time begun,
   May the same homage still be done,
      When earth and heaven itself decays.

*Charity.*

1. Happy the heart, where graces reign,
   Where love inspires the breast;
   Love is the brightest of the train,
   And perfects all the rest.

2. Knowledge, alas! 'tis all in vain,
   And all in vain our fear:
   Our stubborn sins will fight and reign;
   If love be absent there.

3. 'Tis love that makes our cheerful feet
   In swift obedience move:
   The devils know and tremble too;
   But Satan cannot love.

4. This is the grace that lives and sings,
   When faith and hope shall cease:
   'Tis this shall strike our joyful strings
   In the sweet realms of bliss.

5. Yes, ere we quite forsake our clay,
   Or leave this dark abode,
   The wings of love bear us away
   To see our gracious God.

*Unfruitfulness.*

1. Long have I sat beneath the found
   Of thy salvation, Lord;
   But still how weak my faith is found,
   And knowledge of thy word!

C-11

2. Oft I frequent thy holy place,
   Yet hear almost in vain;
   How small a portion of thy grace
   Can my hard heart retain!

3. My gracious Savior and my God,
   How little art thou known
   By all the judgments of thy rod,
   And blessings of thy throne?

4. How cold and feeble is my love!
   How negligent my fear!
   How low my hope of joys above!
   How few affections there!

5. Great God, thy sovereign power impart,
   To give thy word success;
   Write thy salvation on my heart,
   And make me learn thy grace.

6. Shew my forgetful feet the way
   That leads to joy on high,
   Where knowledge grows without decay,
   And love shall never die.

### Sincere Praise.

1. Almighty Maker, God,
   How glorious is thy name!
   Thy wonders how diffus'd abroad
   Throughout creation's frame!

2. In native white and red
   The rose and lily stand,
   And free from pride their beauties spread
   To shew thy skilful hand.

3. The lark mounts up the sky
   With unambitious song,
   And bears her Maker's praise on high
   Upon her artless tongue.

4. Fain would I rise and sing
   To my Creator too;
   Fain would my heart adore my King,
   And give him praises due.

5. But pride, that busy sin,
   Spoils all that I perform,
   Curs'd pride, that creeps securely in,
   And swells a haughty worm.

6. Thy glories I abate,
   Or praise thee with design;
   Part of thy favours I forget,
   Or think the merit mine.

7. Create my soul anew,
   Else all my worship's vain:
   This wretched heart will ne'er prove true
   Till it be form'd again.

8. Descend, celestial fire,
   And seize me from above:
   Wrap me in flames of pure desire,
   A sacrifice to love.

9. Let joy and worship spend
   The remnant of my days,
   And to my God my soul ascend
   In sweet perfumes of praise.

### Christ's Compassion for the Tempted

1. With joy we meditate the grace
   Of our High-Priest above;
   His heart is made of tenderness,
   His bowels melt with love.

2. Touch'd with a sympathy within,
   He knows our feeble frame;
   He knows what sore temptations mean,
   For he hath felt the same.

3. He, in the days of feeble flesh,
   Pour'd out his cries and tears
   And in his measure feels afresh
   What every member bears.

4. He'll never quench the smoking flax,
   But raise it to a flame:
   The bruised reed he never breaks,
   Nor scorns the meanest name.

5. Then let our humble faith address
   His mercy and his power:
   We shall obtain deliv'ring grace
   In the distressing hour.

### The Comparison and Complaint

1. Infinite power, eternal Lord,
   How sov'reign is thy hand!
   All nature rose t' obey thy word,
   And moves at thy command.

2. With steady course the shining sun
   Keeps his appointed way,
   And all the hours obedient run
   The circle of the day.

3. But ah! how wide my spirit flies,
   And wanders from her God!
   My soul forgets the heavenly prise,
   And treads the downward road.

C-12

4. The raging fire and stormy sea
   Perform thy awful will,
   And every beast and every tree
   Thy great design fulfil:

5. While my wild passions rage within,
   Nor thy commands obey;
   But flesh and sense, enslaved to sin,
   Draw my best thoughts away.

6. Shall creatures of a meaner frame
   Pay all their dues to Thee?
   Creatures that never knew thy name,
   That ne'er were lov'd like me?

7. Great God, create my soul anew,
   Conform my heart to thine,
   Melt down my will, and let it flow,
   And take the mould divine.

8. Seize my whole frame into thy hand,
   Here all my powers I bring;
   Manage the wheels by thy command,
   And govern every spring.

9. Then shall my feet no more depart,
   Nor my affections rove;
   Devotion shall be all my heart,
   And all my passions love.

*Breathing after the Holy Spirit.*

1. Come, Holy Spirit, heavenly dove,
   With all thy quick'ning powers,
   Kindle a flame of sacred love
   In these cold hearts of ours.

2. Look how we grovel here below,
   Fond of these earthly toys;
   Our souls, how heavily they go
   To reach eternal joys!

3. In vain we turn our formal songs,
   In vain we strive to rise;
   Hosannas languish on our tongues,
   And our devotion dies.

4. Father, shall we then ever live
   At this poor dying rate?
   Our love so faint, so cold to Thee,
   And thine to us so great?

5. Come, Holy Spirit, heavenly dove,
   With all thy quickening powers;
   Come, shed abroad a Saviour's love,
   And that shall kindle ours.

*The Witnessing Spirit.*

1. Why should the children of a king
   Go mourning all their days?
   Great Comforter, descend, and bring
   The tokens of thy grace.

2. Dost thou not dwell in all thy saints,
   And seal the heirs of heaven?
   When wilt thou banish my complaints,
   And shew my sins forgiven?

3. Assure my conscience of her part
   In the Redeemer's blood;
   And bear thy witness with my heart,
   That I am born of God.

4. Thou art the earnest of his love,
   The pledge of joys to come;
   May thy blest wings, celestial dove,
   Safely convey me home.

*Veni, Creator.*

1. Creator spirit, by whose aid
   The world's foundation first was laid,
   Come visit ev'ry waiting mind;
   Come pour thy joys on human kind;
   From sin and sorrow set us free,
   And make thy temples worthy Thee.

2. O source of uncreated heat,
   The Father's promised Paraclete!
   Thrice holy fount, immortal fire,
   Our hearts with heavenly love inspire;
   Come, and thy sacred unction bring
   To sanctify us while we sing.

3. Plenteous of Grace, descend from high,
   Rich in the seven-fold energy!
   Thou strength of his almighty hand,
   Whose power does heaven and earth command.
   Refine and purege our earthly parts,
   And stamp thine image on our hearts.

4. Create all new, our will control,
   Subdue the rebel in our soul;
   Chase from our mind th' infernal foe,
   And peace the fruit of faith bestow:
   And lest again we go astray,
   Protect and guide us in thy way.

5. Immortal honours, endless fame
   Attend th' Almighty Father's name;
   The Saviour Son be glorified,
   Who for lost man's redemption died:
   And equal adoration be,
   Eternal Comforter, to Thee.

*A Hymn for Sunday.*

1. The Lord of Sabbath let us praise
   In concert with the blest,
   Who joyful in harmonious lays
   Employ an endless rest.

2. Thus, Lord, while we remember thee,
   We blest and pious grow;
   By hymns of praise we learn to be
   Triumphant here below.

3. On this glad day a brighter scene
   Of glory was display'd
   By God, th' Eternal word, than when
   This universe was made.

4. He rises, who mankind has bought
   With grief and pain extreme;
   "Twas great to speak the world from naught,
   "Twas greatest to redeem.

# A COLLECTION OF PSALMS AND HYMNS

## Part the Second.

### PSALM VIII.
*Part the First.*

1. Sovereign, everlasting Lord,
   How excellent thy name!
   Held in being by thy word,
   Thee all thy works proclaim:
   Thro' the earth thy glories shine,
   Thro' those dazzling world's above,
   All confess the source divine,
   Th' almighty God of love!

2. Thou the God of power and grace,
   Whom highest heavens adore,
   Callest babes to sing thy praise,
   And manifest thy power:
   Lo! they in thy strength go on,
   Lo! on all thy foes they tread,
   Cast the dire accuser down,
   And bruise the serpent's head.

3. Yet when I survey the skies
   And planets as they roll,
   Wonder dims my aching eyes,
   And swallows up my soul;
   Moon and stars so wide display,
   Chaunt their Maker's praise so loud,
   Pour insufferable day,
   And draw me up to God!

4. What is man, that thou, O Lord,
   Hast such respect to him!
   Comes from Heaven th' incarnate Word,
   His creature to redeem:
   Wherefore would'st thou stoop so low?
   Who the myst'ry shall explain?
   God is flesh and lives below,
   And dies for wretched man.

*Part the Second.*

1. Jesus, his Redeemer dies,
   The sinner to restore,
   Falls that man again may rise,
   And stand as heretofore:
   Foremost of created things,
   Head of all thy works he stood,
   Nearest the great King of kings,
   And *little less* than God*!

2. Him with glorious majesty
   Thy grace vouchsas'd to crown;
   Transcript of the One in Three,
   He in thine image shone:
   All thy works for him were made,
   All did to his sway submit,
   Fishes, birds, and beasts obey'd,
   And bow beneath his feet.

3. Sovereign, everlasting Lord,
   How excellent thy name!
   Held in being by thy word
   Thee all thy works proclaim:
   Thro' this earth thy glories shine,
   Thro' those dassling worlds above,
   All confess the Source divine,
   Th' almighty God of love!

### PSALM XVIII. *ver. 1, &c.*

1. Thee will I love, O Lord my power:
   My rock and fortress is the Lord,
   My God, my saviour, and my tower,
   My horn and strength, my shield and sword:
   Secure I trust in his defence,
   I stand in his omnipotence.

*So it is in the Hebrew

2. Still will I invocate his name,
  And spend my life in prayer and praise,
His goodness own, his promise claim,
  And look for all his saving grace,
'Till all his saving grace I see,
  From sin and hell for ever free.

3. He sav'd me in temptation's hour,
  Horribly caught and compass'd round,
Expos'd to Satan's raging power,
  In floods of sin and sorrow drown'd,
Condemn'd the second death to feel,
  Arrested by the pains of hell.

4. To God my God with plaintive cry
  I call'd in agony of fear,
My humble wailing pierced the sky,
  My groaning reach'd his gracious ear,
He heard me from his glorious throne,
And sent the timely rescue down.

### PSALM XXIII

1. The Lord my pasture shall prepare,
And feed me with a shepherd's care,
His presence shall my wants supply,
And guard me with a watchful eye;
My noon-day walks he shall attend,
And all my midnight hours defend.

2. When in the sultry glebe I faint,
Or on the thirsty mountains pant,
To fertile vales, and dewy meads
My weary, wand'ring steps he leads;
Where peaceful rivers soft and slow
Amid the verdant landskip flow.

3. Tho' in the paths of death I tread,
With gloomy horrors overspread,
My stedfast heart shall fear no ill,
For thou, O Lord, art with me still;
Thy friendly crook shall give me aid,
And guide me through the dreadful shade.

4. Tho' in a bare and rugged way
Thro' devious, lonely wilds I stray,
Thy bounty my pains shall beguile;
The barren wilderness shall smile,
With sudden greens and herbage crown'd,
And streams shall murmur all around.

### PSALM XXIV.

*Part the First*

1. The earth and all her fulness owns
  Jehovah for her Sovereign Lord;
The countless myriads of her sons
  Rose into being at his word.

2. His word did out of nothing call
  The world, and founded all that is;
Launch'd on the floods this solid ball,
  And fix'd it in the floating seas.

3. But who shall quit this low abode,
  Who shall ascend the heavenly place,
And stand upon the mount of God,
  And see his Maker face to face?

4. The man whose hands and heart are clean,
  That blessed portion shall receive;
Whoe'er by grace is sav'd from sin,
  Hereafter shall in glory live.

5. He shall obtain the starry crown;
  And number'd with the saints above,
The God of his salvation own,
  The God of his salvation love.

6. This is the chosen royal race
  That seek their Saviour God to see,
To see in holiness thy face,
  O Jesus, and be join'd to thee.

*Part the Second.*

1. Thou the true wrestling *Jacob* art,
  Whose prayers, and tears, and blood inclin'd
Thy Father's majesty t' impart
  His name, his love to all mankind.

2. Our Lord is risen from the dead,
  Our Jesus is gone up on high,
The powers of hell are captive led,
  Dragg'd to the portals of the sky.

3. There his triumphal chariot waits,
  And angels chaunt the solemn lay,
Lift up your heads, ye heavenly gates,
  Ye everlasting doors, give way.

4. Loose all your bars of massy light,
  And wide unfold th' etheral scene;
He claims these mansions as his right,
  Receive the King of glory in.

5. Who is the King of glory, who?
    The Lord that all his foes o'ercame;
    The world, sin, death, and hell o'erthrew:
    And Jesus is the conqueror's name.

6. Lo! his triumphal chariot waits,
    And angels chaunt the solemn lay,
    Lift up your heads, ye heavenly gates,
    Ye everlasting doors, give way.

7. Who is the King of glory, who?
    The Lord of glorious power possest,
    The King of saints and angels too,
    God over all, for ever blest.

### PSALM XXXII.

*Part the First.*

1. Blest is the man, supremely blest,
    Whose wickedness is all forgiven,
    Who finds in Jesu's wounds his rest,
    And sees the smiling face of heaven.
    The guilt and power of sin is gone
    From him that doth in Christ believe,
    Cover'd it lies, and still kept down,
    And buried in his Saviour's grave.

2. Blest is the man, to whom his Lord
    No, more imputes iniquity,
    Whose spirit is by race restor'd,
    From all the guile of Satan free;
    Free from design, or selfish aim,
    Blameless and pure and undefil'd,
    A simple follower of the Lamb,
    And harmless as a new-born child.

*Part the Second.*

1. Thou art my hiding place, in thee
    I rest secure from sin and hell,
    Safe in the love that ransom'd me,
    And shelter'd in thy wounds I dwell:
    Still shall thy grace to me abound,
    The countless wonders of thy grace
    I still shall tell to all around,
    And sing my great deliv'rer's praise.

2. Ye faithful souls, rejoice in him
    Whose arms are still your sure defence;
    Your Lord is mighty to redeem:
    Believe: and who shall pluck you thence?
    Ye men of upright heart, be glad,
    For Jesus is your God and friend,
    He keeps whoe'er on him are slay'd,
    And he shall keep them to the end.

### PSALM XXXVI.

1. Thou, O my Lord, art full of grace,
    Above the clouds thy mercies rise,
    Stedfast thy truth and faithfulness,
    Thy word of promise never dies;
    Nor earth can shake, nor hell remove
    The base of thine eternal love.

2. Unsearchable thy judgments are,
    A boundless bottomless abyss:
    But lo! thy providential care
    O'er all thy works extended is;
    In Thee the creatures live, and move,
    And are: All glory to thy love!

3. Thy love sustains the world it made,
    Thy love preserves both man and beast,
    Beneath thy wing's almighty shade
    The sons of men securely rest;
    And those who haunt the hallow'd place,
    Shall banquet on thy richest grace.

4. Their souls shall drink the crystal stream
    Which ever issues from thy throne:
    Fountain of joy and bliss supreme,
    Eternal life and thou are one,
    To us, to all so freely given,
    The light of life, the heaven of heaven.

5. Stay then with those that know thy peace,
    The simple men of heart sincere;
    From all their foes and sins release,
    From pride and lust redeem them here:
    Thine utmost saving grace extend,
    And love, O love them to the end.

### PSALM XLV.
*Part the First*

1. My heart is full of Christ, and longs
    Its glorious matter to declare;
    Of him I make my loftier songs,
    I cannot from his praise forbear;
    My ready tongue makes haste to sing
    The beauties of my heavenly King.

2. Fairer than all the earth-born race,
    Perfect in comeliness Thou art;
    Replenish'd are thy lips with grace,
    And full of love thy tender heart:
    God ever blest, we bow the knee,
    And own all fulness dwells in thee.

3. Gird on thy thigh the Spirit's sword,
     And take to thee thy power divine;
   Stir up thy strength, almighty Lord,
     All power and majesty are thine:
   Assert thy worship and renown,
   O all redeeming God come down.

4. Come, and maintain thy righteous cause,
     And let thy glorious toil succeed;
   Dispread the vict'ry of thy cross,
     Ride on and prosper in thy deed;
   Through earth triumphantly ride on,
   And reign in all our hearts alone.

5. Still let the word of truth prevail,
     The gospel of thy gen'ral grace,
   Of mercy mild that ne'er shall fail,
     Of everlasting righteousness,
   Into the faithful God brought in,
   To root out all the seeds of sin.

### Part the Second.

1. Terrible things thine own right hand
     Shall teach thy greatness to perform:
   Who in the vengeful day can stand
     Unshaken by thine anger's storm,
   While riding on the whirlwind's wings
   They meet the thund'ring King of kings!

2. Sharp are the arrows of thy love,
     And pierce the most obdurate heart:
   Their point thine enemies shall prove,
     And strangely fill'd with pleasing smart,
   Fall down before the cross subdued,
   And feel thine arrows dipt in blood.

3. O God of love, thy sway we own,
     Thy dying love doth all controul;
   Justice and grace support thy throne,
     Set up in every faithful soul;
   Stedfast it stands in them, and sure,
   When pure as thou our God art pure.

4. Thee, Jesus, King of kings and Lord
     Of lords, I glory to proclaim,
   From age to age thy praise record,
     That all the world may learn thy name:
   And all shall soon thy grace adore,
   When time and sin shall be no more.

### PSALM XLVII.

#### Part the First.

1. Clap your hands, ye people all,
   Praise the God on whom we call,
   Lift your voice, and shout his praise,
   Triumph in his sovereign grace.

2. Glorious is the Lord most high,
   Terrible in majesty,
   He his sovereign sway maintains,
   King o'er all the earth he reigns.

3. He the people shall subdue,
   Make us kings and conquerors too,
   Force the nations to submit,
   Bruise our sins beneath our feet.

4. He shall bless his ransom'd ones,
   Number us with Israel's sons;
   God our heritage shall prove,
   Give us all a lot of love.

5. Jesus is gone up on high,
   Takes his seat above the sky:
   Shout the angel quires aloud,
   Echoing to the trump of God.

6. Sons of earth, the triumph join,
   Praise him with the host divine,
   Emulate the heavenly powers,
   Their victorious Lord is ours.

7. Shout the God enthron'd above,
   Trumpet forth his conquering love;
   Praises to our Jesus sing,
   Praises to our glorious King!

#### Part the Second.

1. Pow'r is all to Jesus given,
   Pow'r o'er hell, and earth, and heaven;
   Pow'r he now to us imparts;
   Praise him with believing hearts.

2. Heathens he compels t' obey,
   Saints he rules with mildest sway,
   Pure and holy hearts alone
   Chuses for his quiet throne.

3. Peace to them and power he brings,
   Makes his subjects priests and kings,
   Guards while in his worship join'd,
   Bids them cast the world behind.

C-17

4. On himself he takes their care,
   Saves them not by sword or spear;
   Safely to his house they go,
   Fearless of th' invading foe.

5. God keeps off the hostile bands,
   God protects their happy lands,
   Stands as Keeper of their fields,
   Stands as twice ten thousand shields.

6. Wonderful in saving power,
   Him let all our hearts adore,
   Earth and heaven repeat the cry,
   Glory be to God most high!

### PSALM LVII

1. Be merciful, O God, to me,
   To me who in thy love confide;
   To thy protecting love I flee,
   Beneath thy wings my soul I hide,
   "Till Satan's tyranny is o'er,
   And cruel sin subsists no more.

2. To God will I in trouble cry,
   Who freely undertakes my cause;
   My God most merciful and high
   Shall save me from the lion's jaws,
   Destroy him, ready to devour,
   With all his works and all his power.

3. The Lord out of his holy place
   His mercy and his truth shall send:
   Jesus is full of truth and grace,
   Jesus shall still my soul defend,
   While in the toils of hell I lie,
   And from the den of lions cry.

4. Be thou, exalted, Lord above
   The highest names in earth and heaven;
   Let angels sing thy glorious love,
   And bless the name to sinners given:
   All earth and heaven their king proclaim;
   Bow every knee to Jesu's name.

5. Thee will I praise among thine own;
   Thee will I to the world extol,
   And make thy truth and goodness known;
   Thy goodness, Lord, is over all;
   Thy truth and grace the heavens transcend,
   Thy faithful mercies never end.

6. Be thou exalted, Lord above
   The highest names in earth or heaven;
   Let angels sing thy glorious love,
   And bless the name to sinners given;
   All earth and heaven their king proclaim;
   Bow every knee to Jesu's name.

### PSALM LXXXIV.

1. Lord of the worlds above,
   How pleasant and how fair
   The dwellings of thy love,
   The earthly temples are:
   To thine abode my heart aspires,
   With warm desires to see my God.

2. O happy souls that pray
   Where God appoints to hear!
   O happy men that pay
   Their constant service there!
   They praise Thee still: and happy they
   That love the way to *Sion's* hill.

3. They go from strength to strength
   Thro' the dark vale of tears,
   'Till each o'ercomes at length,
   'Till each in heaven appears:
   O glorious seat! Thou God our King
   Shalt thither bring our willing feet.

4. God is our sun and shield,
   Our light and our defence;
   With gifts his hands are fill'd,
   We draw our blessings thence:
   He shall bestow upon our race
   His saving grace, and glory too.

5. The Lord his people loves,
   His hand no good withholds
   From those his heart approves,
   From holy, humble souls:
   Thrice happy he, O God of hosts,
   Whose spirit trusts alone in Thee.

### PSALM LXXXIX.

1. Thy mercies, Lord, shall be my song,
   My song on them shall ever dwell,
   To ages yet unborn my tongue
   Thy never-failing truth shall tell.

2. For thy stupendous truth and love
   Both heaven and earth just praises owe,
   By quires of angels sung above,
   And by assembled saints below.

3. What seraph of celestial birth
   To vie with *Israel's* God shall dare?
   Or who among the gods of earth
   With our almighty Lord compare?

4. With rev'rence and religious dread
   His servants to his house should press:
   His fear through all their hearts should spread
   Who his almighty name confess.

5. Lord God of armies, who can boast
   Of strength and power, like thine, renown'd?
   Of such a num'rous faithful host
   As that which does thy throne surround?

6. Thou dost the lawless sea controul,
   And change the prospect of the deep;
   Thou mak'st the sleeping billows roll,
   Thou mak'st the rolling billows sleep.

7. In thee the sovereign right remains
   Of earth and heaven: Thee, Lord, alone
   The world and all that it contains,
   Their Maker and Preserver own.

8. Thy arm is mighty, strong thy hand,
   Yet, Lord, thou dost with justice reign:
   Possest of absolute command,
   Thou truth and mercy dost maintain.

### PSALM C.

1. Before Jehovah's awful throne,
   Ye nations, bow with sacred joy:
   Know that the Lord is God alone;
   He can create, and he destroy.

2. His sovereign power, without our aid,
   Made us of clay, and form'd us men;
   And when like wand'ring sheep we stray'd,
   He brought us to his fold again.

3. We'll crowd thy gates with thankful songs,
   High as the heavens our voices raise;
   And earth, with her ten thousand tongues,
   Shall fill thy courts with sounding praise.

4. Wide as the world is thy command,
   Vast as eternity thy love:
   Firm as a rock thy truth must stand,
   When rolling years shall cease to move.

### PSALM CIII.

*Part the First.*

1. My soul inspired with sacred love,
   God's holy name for ever bless;
   Of all his favours mindful prove,
   And still thy grateful thanks express.

2. 'Tis he that all thy sins forgives,
   And after sickness makes thee sound:
   From danger he thy life retrieves,
   By him with grace and mercy crown'd.

3. The Lord abounds with tender love,
   And unexampled acts of grace;
   His waken'd wrath does slowly move,
   His willing mercy flies apace.

4. As high as heaven its arch extends
   Above this little spot of clay;
   So much his boundless love transcends
   The small regards that we can pay.

*Part the Second.*

1. As far as 'tis from east to west,
   So far hath he our sins remov'd;
   Who, with a father's tender breast,
   Hath such as fear'd him always lov'd.

2. The Lord, the universal King,
   In heaven hath fix'd his lofty throne:
   To him, ye angels, praises sing,
   In whose great strength his praise is shewn.

3. Ye that his just commands obey,
   And hear and do his sacred will,
   Ye host of his, this tribute pay,
   Who still what he ordains fulfil.

4. Let every creature jointly bless
   The mighty Lord: And thou, my heart,
   With grateful joy thy thanks express,
   And in this concert bear thy part.

### PSALM CIV.

*Part the First.*

1. Bless God, my soul: Thou, Lord, alone
   Possessest empire without bounds;
   With honour thou art crown'd: thy throne
   Eternal majesty surrounds.

2. With light thou dost thyself enrobe,
   And glory for a garment take,
   Heaven's curtains stretch beyond the globe,
   Thy canopy of state to make.

3. God builds on liquid air, and forms
   His palace chamber in the skies;
   The clouds his chariots are, and storms
   The swift wing'd steeds on which he flies.

4. As bright as flame, as swift as wind,
   His ministers heaven's palace fill,
   To have their sundry talks assign'd,
   All pleas'd to serve their sovereign's will.

5. Earth, on her centre fix'd, he set,
   Her face with waters overspread;
   Nor proudest mountains dar'd, as yet,
   To lift above the waves their head.

6. But when thy awful face appear'd,
   Th' insulting waves dispers'd; they fled,
   When once thy thunder's voice they heard,
   And by their haste confess'd their dread.

7. Thence up by secret tracks they creep,
   And gushing from the mountain's side,
   Thro' valleys travel to the deep,
   Appointed to receive their tide.

8. There hail thou fix'd the ocean's bounds,
   The threatening surges to repel.
   That they no more o'erpass their bounds,
   Nor to a second deluge swell.

*Part the Second.*

1. Yet thence in smaller parties drawn,
   The sea recovers her lost hills;
   And starting springs from every lawn
   Surprise the vale with plenteous rills.

2. The fields, tame beasts are thither led,
   Weary with labour, faint with drought;
   And asses on wild mountains bred,
   Have sense to find these currents out.

3. There shady trees from scorching beams
   Yield shelter to the feather'd throng;
   They drink, and for the bounteous streams,
   Return the tribute of their song.

4. Thy rains from heav'n-parch'd hills recruit,
   That soon transmit the liquid store,
   'Till earth is burthen'd with her fruit,
   And nature's lap can hold no more.

5. Grass, for our cattle to devour,
   Thou mak'st the growth of every field;
   Herbs for man's use of various power,
   That either food or physic yield.

6. With cluster'd grapes he crowns the vine,
   To cheer man's heart oppress'd with cares;
   Gives oil, that makes his face to shine,
   And corn, that wasted strength, repairs.

*Part the Third.*

1. The trees of God, without the care
   Or art of man, with sap are fed;
   The mountain-cedar looks as fair
   As those in royal gardens bred.

2. Safe in the lofty cedar's arms
   The wand'rers of the air may rest;
   The hospitable pine from harms
   Protects the stork, her pious guest.

3. Wild goats the craggy rock ascend,
   In tow'ring heights their fortress make,
   Whose cells in labyrinths extend,
   Where feebler creatures refuge take.

4. The moon's inconstant aspect shows,
   Th' appointed seasons of the year;
   Th' instructed sun his duty knows,
   His hour to rise, and disappear.

5. Darkness he makes the earth to shroud,
   When forest-beasts securely stray;
   Young lions roar their wants aloud
   To Providence that sends them prey.

6. They range all night on slaughter bent,
   'Til summoned by the rising morn,
   To sculk in dens, with one consent,
   The conscious ravagers return.

7. Forth to the tillage of the soil
   The husbandman securely goes,
   Commencing with the sun his toil,
   With him returns to his repose.

8. How various, Lord, thy works are found,
   For which thy wisdom we adore;
   The earth is with thy treasure crown'd,
   'Till nature's hand can grasp no more.

*Part the Fourth.*

1. But still the vast unfathom'd main
   Of wonders a new scene supplies,
   Whole depth inhabitants contain
   Of every form and every size.

2. Full-freighted ships from every port
   There cut their unmolested way;
   Leviathan, whom there to sport
   Thou mad'st, hath compass there to play.

3. These various troops of sea and land
   In sense of common want agree;
   All wait on thy dispensing hand,
   And have their daily alms of thee.

C-20

4. They gather what thy stores disperse
Without their trouble to provide;
Thou op'st thy hand, the universe,
The craving world is all supplied.

5. Thou for a moment hid'st thy face,
The num'rous ranks of creatures mourn;
Thou tak'st their breath, all nature's race
Forthwith to mother-earth return.

6. Again thou send'st thy spirit forth,
T' inspire the mass with vital feed;
Nature restor'd, and parent-earth
Smiles on her new-created breed.

7. Thus thro' successive ages stands
Firm fix'd thy providential care;
Pleas'd with the work of thine own hands,
Thou dost the wastes of time repair.

8. One look of thine, one wraithful look,
Earth's panting breast with terrors fills;
One touch from Thee, with clouds of smoke
In darkness shrouds the proudest hills.

9. In praising God, while he prolongs
My breath, I will that breath employ,
And join devotion to my songs,
Sincere as is in him my joy.

10. While sinners from earth's face are hurl'd,
My soul, praise thou his holy name,
'Till with my song the listening world
Join concert, and his praise proclaim.

## PSALM CXIII

1. Ye saints and servants of the Lord,
The triumphs of his Name record,
His sacred Name for ever bless;
Where'er the circling sun displays
His rising beams or setting rays,
Due praise to his great Name address.

2. God thro' the world extends his way,
The regions of eternal day
But shadows of his glory are:
With him, whose majesty excels,
Who made the heaven in which he dwells,
Let no created power compare.

3. Tho' 'tis beneath his state to view
In highest heaven what angels do,
Yet he to earth vouchsafes his care;
He takes the needy from his cell,
Advancing him in courts to dwell
Companion of the greatest there.

4. To Father, Son, and Holy Ghost,
The God whom heaven's triumphant host
And suff'ring saints on earth adore,
Be glory as in ages past,
As now it is, and so shall last
When earth and heaven shall be no more.

## PSALM CXIV.

1. When *Israel* freed from *Pharoah's* hand,
Left the proud tyrant and his land,
The tribes with cheerful homage own
Their King; and *Judah* was his throne.

2. Across the deep their journey lay;
The deep divides to make them way:
*Jordan* beheld their march, and fled
With backward current to his head.

3. The mountains shook like frighted sheep;
Like lambs the little hillocks leap:
Not *Sinai* on his base could stand,
Conscious of sovereign power at hand.

4. What power could make the deep divide?
Make *Jordan* backward roll his tide?
Why did ye leap, ye little hills?
And whence the fright that *Sinai* feels?

5. Let every mountain, every flood
Retire, and know th' approaching God,
The king of *Israel*: see him here!
Tremble thou earth; adore and fear!

6. He thunders, and all nature mourns;
The rock to standing pools he turns:
Flints spring with fountains at his word,
And fires and seas confess the Lord.

### *The Same.*

1. When *Israel* out of *Egypt* came,
And left the proud oppressor's land,
Conducted by the great I AM,
Safe in the hollow of his hand;
The Lord in *Israel* reign'd alone,
And *Judah* was his fav'rite throne.

2. The sea beheld his power, and fled,
Disparted by the wondrous rod;
*Jordan* ran backward to his head,
And *Sinai* felt th' incumbent God:
The mountains skip'd like frighted rams,
The hills leap'd after them as lambs.

3. What ail'd thee, O thou trembling sea?
　　What horror turn'd the river back?
Was nature's God, displeas'd at thee?
　　And why shall hills and mountains shake?
Ye mountains huge, who skip'd like rams,
Ye hills who leap'd as frighted lambs?

4. Earth tremble on, with all thy sons,
　　In presence of thy awful Lord,
Whose power inverted nature owns,
　　Her only law his sovereign word:
He shakes the centre with his nod,
And heaven bows down to *Jacob's* God.

5. Creation, varied by his hand,
　　Th' omnipotent Jehovah knows;
The sea is turn'd to solid land,
　　The rock into a fountain flows;
And all things, as they change, proclaim
Their Lord eternally the same.

### PSALM CXVI.

1. O Thou, who when I did complain,
　　Didst all my griefs remove,
O Saviour, do not now disdain
　　My humble praise and love.

2. Since thou a pitying ear didst give,
　　And heard me when I pray'd,
I'll call upon thee while I live,
　　And never doubt thy aid.

3. Pale death with all his ghastly train
　　My soul encompast round;
Anguish, and sin, and death, and pain,
　　On every side I found.

4. To thee, O Lord of life, I pray'd,
　　And did for succor flee;
O save (in my distress I said)
　　The soul that trusts in thee.

5. How good thou art, how large thy grace!
　　How easy to forgive!
The helpless thou delight'st to raise;
　　And by thy love I live.

6. Then, O my soul, be never more
　　With anxious thoughts disrest;
God's bounteous love doth thee restore
　　To ease, and joy, and rest.

7. My eyes no longer drown'd in tears,
　　My feet from falling free,
Redeem'd from death and guilty fears,
　　O Lord, I'll live to thee.

### PSALM CXVII.

1. Ye Nations, who the globe divide,
　　Ye num'rous nations scatter'd wide,
　　　To God your grateful voices raise:
To all his boundless mercies shown,
His truth to endless ages known,
　　　Require our endless love and praise.

2. To him who reigns enthron'd on high,
　　To his dear Son who deign'd to die,
　　　Our guilt and errors to remove;
To that blest Spirit who grace imparts,
Who rules in all believing hearts,
　　　Be ceaseless glory, praise, and love.

### PSALM CXVIII.
#### *Part the First.*

1. All glory to our gracious Lord;
　　His love be by his church ador'd,
　　　His love eternally the same:
His love let *Aaron's* sons confess,
His free, and everlasting grace
　　　Let all that fear the Lord proclaim.

2. In trouble on the Lord I cried,
　　And felt the pard'ning word applied:
　　　He answer'd me in peace and power,
He pluck'd my soul out of the net,
In a large place of safety set,
　　　And bad me go and sin no more.

3. The Lord, I now can say, is mine;
　　And confident in strength divine,
　　　Nor man, nor fiends, nor flesh I fear:
Jesus the Saviour takes my part,
And keeps the issues of my heart;
　　　My Helper is for ever near.

4. Better it is in God to trust,
　　In God the good, the strong, the just,
　　　Than a false, sinful child of man;
Better in Jesus to confide
Than every other prince beside,
　　　Who offer all their helps in vain.

#### *Part the Second.*

1. O Sin my cruel bosom-foe,
　　Oft hast thou sought my soul t' o'erthrow,
　　　And surely thrust at me in vain:
In my defence the Saviour stood,
Cover'd with his victorious blood,
　　　And arm'd my sprinkled heart again.

2. Righteous I am in him, and strong,
   He is become my joyful song,
     My Saviour and Salvation too:
   I triumph thro' his mighty grace,
   And pure in heart shall see his face,
     And rise in Christ's creature new.

3. The voice of joy, and love, and praise,
   And thanks for his redeeming grace,
     Among the justified is found:
   With songs that rival those above,
   With shouts proclaiming Jesu's love,
     Both day and night their tents resound.

4. The Lord's right-hand hath wonders wrought
   Above the reach of human thought,
     The Lord's right-hand exalted is;
   We see it still stretch'd out to save,
   The power of God in Christ we have,
     And Jesus is the Prince of peace.

### Part the Third.

1. I shall not die in sin, but live,
   To Christ my Lord, the glory give,
     His miracles of grace declare;
   When he the work of faith hath done;
   When I have put his image on,
     And fruit unto perfection bear.

2. The Lord hath sorely chasten'd me,
   And bruis'd for mine iniquity,
     Yet mercy would not give me up;
   Caught from the jaws of second death,
   Pluck'd out of the devourer's teeth,
     He bids me now rejoice in hope.

3. Open the gates of righteousness,
   Receive me into Christ my peace,
     That I his praises may record:
   He is the truth, the life, the way,
   The portal of eternal day;
     The gate of heaven is Christ my Lord.

4. Thro' him the just shall enter in,
   Sav'd to the uttermost from sin;
     Already sav'd from all its power:
   The Lord my righteousness I praise,
   And calmly wait the perfect grace,
     When born of God I sin no more.

### Part the Fourth.

1. Jesus is lifted up on high;
   Whom man refus'd and doom'd to die,
     He is become the corner-stone:
   Head of his Church he lives and reigns,
   His kingdom over all maintains,
     High on his everlasting throne.

2. The Lord th' amazing work hath wrought,
   Hath from the dead our shepherd brought,
     Reviv'd on the third glorious day:
   This is the day our God hath made,
   The day for sinners to be glad
     In him who bears their sins away.

3. Thee, Lord, with joyful lips we praise;
   Now, send us now thy saving grace,
     Make this the acceptable hour:
   Our hearts would now receive thee in;
   Enter, and make an end of sin,
     And bless us with the perfect power.

4. Bless us, that we may call thee blest,
   Sent down from heaven to give us rest,
     Thy gracious Father to proclaim,
   His sinless nature to impart;
   In every new, believing heart
     To manifest his glorious name.

5. God is the Lord that shews us light;
   Then let us render him his right,
     The off'ring of a thankful mind;
   Present our living sacrifice,
   And to his cross in closest ties
     With cords of love our spirit bond,

6. Thou art my God, and Thee I praise;
   Thou art my God, I sing thy grace,
     And call mankind t' extol thy name:
   All glory to our gracious Lord,
   His name be prais'd, his love ador'd
     Thro' all eternity the same.

### PSALM CXXI.

1. To the hills I lift mine eyes,
     The everlasting hills;
   Streaming thence in fresh supplies,
     My soul the spirit feels:
   Will he not his help afford?
     Help, while yet I ask, is given;
   God comes down, the God and Lord
     That made both earth and heaven.

2. Faithful souls, pray always; pray,
     And still in God confide;
   He thy feeble steps shall stay,
     Nor suffer thee to slide:
   Lean on the Redeemer's breast,
     He thy quiet spirit keeps:
   Rest in him, securely rest;
     Thy watchman never sleeps.

3. Neither sin, nor earth, nor hell
    Thy Keeper can surprise;
Careless slumber cannot steal
    On his all-seeing eyes:
He is *Israel's* sure defence;
    *Israel* all his care shall prove,
Kept by watchful providence
    And ever-waking love.

4. See the Lord thy Keeper stand
    Omnipotently near:
Lo! He holds thee by thy hand,
    And banishes thy fear;
Shadows with his wings thy head,
    Guards from all impending harms;
Round thee and beneath are spread
    The everlasting arms.

5. Christ shall bless thy going out,
    Shall bless thy coming in,
Kindly compass thee about,
    Till thou art sav'd from sin;
Like thy spotless Master thou,
    Fill'd with wisdom, love, and power,
Holy, pure, and perfect now,
    Hencefore and evermore.

## PSALM CXXV.

1. Who in the Lord confide,
    And feel his sprinkled blood,
In storms and hurricanes abide
    Firm as the mount of God:
    Stedfast, and fixt, and sure
    His *Sion* cannot move,
His faithful people stand secure
    In Jesu's guardian love.

2. As round *Jerusalem*
    The hilly bulwarks rise,
So God protects and covers them
    From all their enemies:
    On every side he stands,
    And for his *Israel* cares,
And safe in his almighty hands
    Their souls for ever-bears.

3. For lo! the reign of hell
    And hellish men is o'er;
They can persuade, they can compel
    The just to sin no more:
    To devils, men, or sin,
    They need no more give place,
Nor ever touch the thing unclean
    When cleans'd by pard'ning grace.

4. But let them still abide
    In Thee, all-gracious Lord,
Till every soul is sanctify'd,
    And perfectly restor'd,
    The men of heart sincere
    Continue to defend,
And do them good, and save them here,
    And love them to the end.

## PSALM CXXVI

1. When our redeeming Lord
    Pronounc'd the pard'ning word,
Turn'd our soul's captivity,
    O what sweet surprise we found!
Wonder ask'd "and can it be!"
    Scarce believ'd the welcome sound.

2. And is it not a dream?
    And are we sav'd thro' him?
Yes, our bounding heart replied,
    Yes, broke out our joyful tongue,
Freely we are justify'd;
    This the new, the gospel song.

3. The heathen too could see
    Our glorious liberty:
All our foes were forc'd to own
    "God for them hath wonders wrought:"
Wonders be for us hath done,
    From the house of bondage brought.

4. To us our gracious God
    His pard'ning love hath shew'd:
Now our joyful souls are free
    From the guilt and power of sin;
Greater things we soon shall see,
    We shall soon be pure within.

5. Turn us again, O Lord,
    Pronounce the second word,
Loose our hearts, and let us go
    Down the spirit 's fullest flood,
Freely to the fountain flow,
    All be swallow'd up in God.

6. Who for thy coming wait,
    And wail their lost estate,
Poor, and sad, and empty still,
    Who for full redemption weep,
They shall thy appearing feel,
    Sow in tears, in joy to reap.

7. Who seed immortal bears,
    And wets his path with tears,
Doubtless he shall soon return,
    Bring his sheaves with vast increase,
Fully of the spirit born,
    Perfected in holiness.

## PSALM CXXVIII

1. Blest is the man that fears the Lord,
    And walks in all his ways,
    An earnest of his great reward
        On earth his Master pays.

2. Thou shalt not spend thy strength in vain
        For perishable food,
    Thy father shall his own sustain,
        And all thy soul with good.

3. Happy in him thy soul shall be,
        And on his fulness feed;
    Jesus who came from heaven for thee,
        Shall be thy living bread.

4. Thy wife shall as the fruitful vine
        Her blooming offspring shew;
    Thy children shall be God's, not thine,
        His pleasant plants below.

5. Around thy plentous tale spread
        Like olive-branches fair,
    Heaven-ward they in thy steps shall tread,
        And meet their parents there.

6. Thus shall the man be blest who owns
        His Maker for his Lord;
    Or doubly blest with better sons
        Begotten by the word.

7. The children of thy faith and prayer
        Thy joyful eyes shall see,
    Shall see the prosp'rous church, and share
        In her prosperity.

8. *Sion* again shall lift her head,
        And flourish all thy days;
    Thy soul shall see the faithful seed,
        And bless the rising race.

9. Fill'd with abiding peace divine,
        With *Israel's* blessing blest,
    Thou then the church above shalt join,
        And gain the heavenly rest.

## PSALM CXXXI.

1. Lord, if thou the grace impart,
    Poor in spirit, meek in heart,
    I shall as my master be,
    Rooted in humility.

2. From the time that thee I know,
    Nothing shall I seek below,
    Aim at nothing great or high,
    Lowly both my heart and eye:

3. Simple, teachable, and mild,
    Aw'd into a little child;
    Quiet now without my food,
    Wean'd from every creature-good.

4. Hangs my new-born soul on thee,
    Kept from all idolatry;
    Nothing wants beneath, above,
    Happy, happy, in thy love.

5. O that all might seek and find
    Every good in Jesus join'd.
    Him let *Israel* still adore,
    Trust him, praise him evermore.

## PSALM CXXXII.

1. Remember, Lord, the pious Zeal
        Of every soul that cleaves to thee,
    The troubles for thy sake they feel,
        Their eager hopes they house to see;
    Their vows to cry and never rest,
        Till thou art in thy church ador'd,
    And dwell'st in every faithful breast,
        And count'st them worthy of their Lord.

2. Arise, O Lord, into thy rest,
        Thou and thy ark of perfect power:
    God over all, for ever blest,
        Thee, Jesus, let our hearts adore.
    Thy priests be cloth'd with righteousness,
        Thy praise their happy lives employ,
    The saint in thee their all posses,
        And shout the sons of God for joy.

## PSALM CXXXIII.
### Part the First.

1. Behold how good a thing
        It is to dwell in peace,
    How pleasing to our king
        This fruit of righteousness:
    When brethren all in one agree,
    Who knows the joys of unity!

2. When all are sweetly join'd,
    (True followers of the Lamb,
    The same in heart and mind)
    And think and speak the same,
And all in love together dwell,
The comfort is unspeakable.

3. Where unity takes place,
    The joys of heaven we prove,
    This is he gospel grace,
    The unction from above:
The spirit on all believers shed,
Descending swift from Christ our head.

4. Where unity is found,
    The sweet anointing grace
    Extends to all around
    And consecrates the place;
To every waiting soul it comes,
And fills it with divine perfumes.

*Part the Second.*

1. Grace every morning new,
    And every night we feel
    The soft refreshing dew,
    That falls from *Hermon's* hill;
On Sion it does sweetly fall,
The grace of one descends on all.

2. Even now our Lord doth pour
    The blessing from above,
    A kindly, gracious shower
    Of heart-reviving love,
The former and the latter rain,
The love of God, and love of man.

3. In him when brethren join,
    And follow after peace,
    The fellowship divine
    He promises to bless,
His chiefest graces to bestow,
Where two or three are met below.

4. The riches of his grace
    In fellowship are given
    To *Sion's* chosen race,
    The citizens of heaven;
He fills them with his choicest store,
He gives them life for evermore.

## PSALM CXXXIV.

1. Ye servants of God, whose diligent care
   Is ever employ'd in watching and prayer,
   With praises unceasing your Jesus proclaim,
   Rejoicing and blessing his excellent name.

2. 'Tis Jesus commands, come all to his house,
   And lift up your hands, and pay him your vows;
   And while ye are giving your Maker his due,
   The Lord out of heaven shall sanctify you.

## PSALM CXXXIX

*Part the First.*

1. Thou, Lord, by strictest search hast known
   My rising up and lying down;
   My secret thoughts are known to thee,
   Known long before conceiv'd by me.

2. Thine eye my bed and path surveys,
   My public haunts, and private ways:
   Thou know'st what 'tis my lips would vent,
   My yet unutter'd words' intent.

3. Surrounded by thy power I stand;
   On every side I find thy hand:
   O skill, for human reach too high!
   Too dazzling bright for mortal eye!

4. O could I so perfidious be,
   To think of once deserting thee;
   Where, Lord, could I thy influence shun,
   Or whether from thy presence run?

5. If up to heaven I take my flight,
   'Tis there thou dwell'st enthron'd in light:
   If down to hell's infernal plains,
   'Tis there almighty vengeance reigns.

6. If I the morning's wings could gain,
   And fly beyond the western main;
   Thy swifter hand would first arrive,
   And there arrest thy fugitive.

7. Or should I try to shun thy sight
   Beneath the sable wings of night;
   One glance from thee, one piercing ray,
   Would kindle darkness into day.

8. The veil of night is no disguise,
   No screen from thy all-searching eyes;
   Thro' midnight shadow thou find'st the way
   As in the blazing noon of day.

C-26

*Part the Second.*

1. Thou know'st the texture of my heart,
   My reins, and every vital part:
   Each single thread in nature's loom
   By thee was cover'd in the womb.

2. I'll prise thee, from whose hands I came
   A work of such a curious frame:
   The wonders thou in me hast shewn,
   My soul with grateful joy shall own.

3. Thine eye my substance did survey,
   While yet a lifeless mass it lay;
   In secret how exactly wrought,
   Ere from its dark enclosure brought.

4. Thou didst the shapeless embryo see,
   It parts were register'd by thee;
   Thou saw'st the daily growth they took,
   Form'd by the model of thy book.

5. Let me acknowledge too, O God,
   That since the maze of life I trod,
   Thy thoughts of love to me surmount
   The power of numbers to recount.

6. Search, try, O Lord, my reins and heart,
   If evil lurk in any part;
   Correct me where I go astray,
   And guide me in thy perfect way.

PSALM CXLV. Ver. 7, &c.

*Part the First.*

1. Sweet is the mem'ry of thy grace,
   My God, my heavenly King;
   Let age to age thy righteousness
   In sounds of glory sing.

2. God reigns on high, but not confines
   His goodness to the skies;
   Thro' the whole earth his goodness shines,
   And every want supplies.

3. With longing eye thy creatures wait
   On thee for daily food;
   Thy lib'ral hand provides them meat,
   And fills their mouths with good.

4. How kind are thy compassions, Lord!
   How slow thine anger moves!
   But soon he sends his pard'ning word,
   To cheer the soul he loves.

5. Creatures, with all their endless race,
   Thy power and praise proclaim;
   But we, who taste thy richer grace,
   Delight to bless thy name.

*Part the Second.* Ver. 14, &c.

1. Let every tongue thy goodness speak,
   Thou sovereign Lord of all:
   Thy strengthening hands uphold the weak,
   And raise the poor that fall.

2. When sorrow bows the spirit down,
   Or virtue lies distrest
   Beneath the proud oppressor's frown,
   Thou giv'st the mourner rest.

3. The Lord supports our infant days,
   And guides our giddy youth:
   Holy and just are all thy ways,
   And all thy words are truth.

4. Thou know'st the pains thy servants feel,
   Thou hear'st thy children cry,
   And their best wishes to fulfil
   Thy grace is ever night.

5. Thy mercy never shall remove
   From men of heart sincere;
   Thou sav'st the souls whose humble love
   Is join'd with holy fear.

6. My lips shall dwell upon thy praise,
   And spread thy fame abroad:
   Let all the sons of *Adam* raise
   The honours of their God.

PSALM CXLVI.

1. I'll praise my Maker while I've breath,
   And when my voice is lost in death,
   Praise shall employ my nobler powers;
   My days of praise shall ne'er be past,
   While life and thought and being last,
   Or immortality endures.

2. Happy the man whose hopes rely
   On *Israel's* God: He made the sky,
   And earth, and seas, with all their train:
   His truth for ever stands secure,
   He save the opprest, he feeds the poor,
   And none shall find his promise vain.

3. The Lord pours eye-sight on the blind;
   The Lord supports the fainting mind;
   He sends the labouring conscience peace,
   He helps the stranger in distress,
   The widow and the fatherless,
   And grants the prisoner sweet release.

4. I'll praise him while he lends me breath
And when my voice is lost in death,
   Praise shall employ my nobler powers;
My days of praise shall ne'er be past,
While life andthought and being last
   Or immortality endures.

### PSALM CXLVII

1. Praise ye the Lord; 'tis good to raise
Our hearts and voices in his praise;
His nature and his works invite
To make this duty our delight.

2. He form'd the stars, those heavenly flames,
He counts their numbers, calls their names:
His wisdom's vast, and knows no bound,
A deep where all our thoughts are drown'd.

3. Great is the Lord, and great his might,
And all his glories infinite:
He crowns the meek, rewards the just,
And treads the wicked to the dust.

4. Sing to the Lord, exalt him high,
Who spreads his clouds around the sky;
There he prepares the fruitful rain,
Nor lets the drops descend in vain.

5. He makes the grass the hills adorn,
And clothes the smiling fields with corn:
The beasts with food his hands supply,
And the young ravens when they cry.

6. What is the creature's skill or force?
The sprightly man or warlike horse?
The piercing wit, the active limb,
All are too mean delights for him.

7. But saints are lovely in his sight,
He views his children with delight;
He sees their hope, he knows their fear,
And looks and loves his image there.

8. Praise God from whom all blessings flow;
Praise him all creatures here below;
Praise him above, ye heavenly host;
Praise Father, Son and Holy Ghost!

### PSALM CXLVIII.
*Part the First.*

1. Let every creature join
   To praise th' eternal God;
Ye heavenly hosts, the song begin,
   And sound his name abroad.

2. The sun, with golden beams,
   And moon with paler rays,
Ye starry lights, ye sparkling flames,
   Shine to your Maker's praise.

3. He built those worlds above,
   And fix'd their wondrous frame;
By his command they stand or move,
   And ever speak his name.

4. Ye vapours, when ye rise,
   Or fall in show'rs or snow;
Ye thunders murm'ring round the skies,
   His power and glory shew.

5. Wind, hail, and flashing fire,
   Agree to praise the Lord,
When ye in vengeful storms conspire
   To execute his word.

6. By all his works above
   His honours be exprest:
But those who taste his saving love,
   Should sing his praises best.

*Part the Second.*

1. Let earth and ocean know,
   They owe their Maker praise:
Praise him, ye wat'ry world below,
   And monsters of the seas.

2. From mountains near the sky
   Let his loud praise resound;
From humble shrubs, and cedars high,
   And vales and fields around.

3. Ye lions of the wood,
   And tamer bests that graze,
Ye live upon his daily food,
   And he expects your praise.

4. Ye birds of lofty wing,
   On high his praises bear,
Or sit on flowery boughs, and sing
   Your Maker's glory there.

5. Ye creeping ants and worms,
   His various wisdom flow:
And flies, in all your shining forms
   Praise him that drest you to:

6. By all the earth-born race
   His honour be express'd:
But those that know his heavenly grace,
   Should learn to praise him best.

*Part the Third.*

1. Monarchs of wide command,
    Praise ye th' eternal King;
 Judges, adore that sovereign hand,
    Whence all your honours spring.

2. Let vig'rous youth engage
    To sound his praises high;
 While growing babes andwith'ring age
    Their feeble voices try.

3. United zeal be shewn,
    His wondrous fame to raise;
 God is the Lord; his name alone
    Deserves our endless praise.

4. Let nature join with art,
    And both pronounce him blest;
 But saints, who dwell so near his heart,
    Should sing his praises best.

*The same.*

1. Ye boundless realms of joy,
    Exalt your Maker's fame;
 His praise your songs employ,
    Above the starry frame.
 Your voices raise, ye cherubim
 And seraphim, to sing his praise.

2. Let them adore the Lord,
    And praise his holy name,
 By whose almighty word
    They all from nothing came;
 And all shall last from changes free:
 His firm decree stands ever fast.

3. Thou moon, that rul'st the night,
    And sun, that guid'st the day,
 Ye glit'ring stars of light,
    To him your homage pay:
 His praise declare, ye heavens above;
 And clouds that move in liquid air.

4. Let earth her tribute pay:
    Praise him, ye dreaded whales,
 And fish that through the sea
    Glide swift with glitt'ring scales;
 Fire, hail, and snow, and misty air,
 And winds that where he bids them blow.

5. By hills and grateful mountains (all
    In grateful concert join'd);
 By cedars stately tall,
    And trees for fruit design'd:
 By every beast and creeping thing,
 And fowl of wing, his name be blest.

6. Let all of royal birth,
    With those of humble frame,
 And judges of the earth,
    His matchless prise proclaim:
 In this design let youth with maids,
 And hoary heads with children join.

7. United zeal be shewn,
    His wondrous fame to raise,
 Whose glorious name alone
    Deserves our endless praise,
 Earth's utmost ends his power obey,
 His glorious sway the sky transcends.

8. His chosen saints to grace
    He sets them up on high
 And favours all their race
    Whose hearts to him are nigh:
 O therefore raise your grateful voice,
 And still rejoice your Lord to praise.

*The Same.*

1. Ye, who dwell above the skies,
    Free from human miseries;
 Ye, whom highest heaven embowers,
    Praise the Lord with all your powers.

2. Angels, your clear voices raise;
    Him ye heavenly armies praise;
 Sun, and moon with borrow'd light,
    All ye sparkling eyes of night.

3. Let the earth his praise resound;
    Monstrous whales, and seas profound;
 Vapours, lightning, hail and snow,
    Storms, which where he bids you, blow:

4. Flowery hills and mountains high;
    Cedars, neighbours to the sky;
 Trees and cattle, creeping things;
    All that cut the air with wings:

5. You who awful sceptres sway;
    You, accustom's to obey;
 Princes, judges of the earth:
    All of high and mumble birth;

6. Youths and virgins flourishing
    In the beauty of your spring;
 Ye, who were but born of late;
    Ye who bow with age's weight:

7. Praise his name with one consent:
    O how great! how excellent!
 Than the earth profounder far;
    Higher than the highest star.

8. He will his to glory raise;
   Ye, his saints, resound his praise;
   Ye, his sons, his chosen race,
   Bless his love and sovereign grace.

*the Same.*

1. Praise ye the Lord, y' immortal quire,
   That fill the realms above;
   Praise him who form'd you of his fire,
   And feeds you with his love.

2. Shine to his praise, ye chrystal skies,
   The floor of his abode;
   Or veil in shades your thousand eyes
   Before your brighter God.

3. Thou restless globe of golden light,
   Whose beams create our days,
   Join with the silver queen of night,
   To own your borrow'd rays.

4. Winds, ye shall bear his name aloud
   Thro' the etherial blue;
   For when his chariot is a cloud,
   He makes his wheels of you.

5. Thunder and hail, and fires and storms,
   The troops of his command,
   Appear in all your dreadful forms,
   And speak his awful hand.

6. Shout to the Lord, ye surging seas,
   In your eternal roar;
   Let wave to wave resound his praise,
   And shore reply to shore:

7. While monsters sporting on the flood,
   In scaly silver shine,
   Speak terribly their maker God,
   And lash the foaming brine.

8. But gentler things shall tune his name
   To softer notes than these,
   Young zephyrs breathing o'er the stream,
   Or whisp'ring thro' the trees.

9. Wave your tall heads, ye lofty pines,
   To him that bids you grow:
   Sweet clusters bend their fruitful vines
   On ev'ry thankful bough.

10. Let the shrill birds his honours raise,
    And climb the morning sky;
    While groveling beasts attempt his praise
    In hoarser harmony.

11. Thus while the meaner creatures sing,
    Ye mortals, take the sound;
    Echo the glories of your King
    Thro' all the nations round.

PSALM CL.

1. Praise the Lord, who reigns above,
   And keeps his court below;
   Praise the holy God of love,
   And all his greatness shew:
   Praise him for his noble deeds,
   Praise him for his matchless power;
   Him, from whom all good proceeds,
   Let earth and heaven adore.

2. Publish, spread to all around
   The great Jehovah's name;
   Let the trumpet's martial sound
   The Lord of Hosts proclaim:
   Praise him every tuneful string,
   All the reach of heavenly art,
   All the powers of music bring
   The music of the heart.

3. Him, in whom they move and live,
   Let every creature sing;
   Glory to their Maker give,
   And homage to their King:
   Hallow'd be his name beneath,
   As in heaven on earth ador'd;
   Praise the Lord in every breath;
   Let all things praise the Lord.

*Hymn to* GOD *the* FATHER.

1. Hail, Father, whose creating call
   Unnumber'd worlds attend,
   Jehovah comprehending all,
   Whom none can comprehend.

2. In light unsearchable enthron'd,
   Which angels dimly see;
   The fountain of the Godhead own'd,
   And foremost of the Three.

3. From thee thro' an eternal Now,
   Thy Son, thine Offspring flow'd;
   An everlasting Father thou,
   As everlasting God;

4. Nor quite display'd to worlds above,
   Nor quite on earth conceal'd;
   By wondrous, unexhausted love
   To mortal man reveal'd.

C-30

5. Supreme and all-sufficient God,
   When nature shall expire;
   And world created by thy nod
   Shall perish by thy fire.

6. Thy name, Jehovah, be ador'd
   By creatures without end,
   Whom none but thy essential word
   And Spirit comprehend.

*Hymn to* GOD *the* SON.

1. Hail, God the Son, in glory crown'd
   Ere time began to be;
   Thron'd with thy Sire thro' half the round
   Of wide eternity.

2. Let heaven and earth's stupendous frame
   Display their Author's power,
   And each exalted seraph-flame,
   Creator, thee adore.

3. Thy wondrous love the Godhead shew'd
   Contracted to a span,
   The co-eternal Son of God.
   The mortal Son of man.

4. To save mankind from lost estate,
   Behold his life-blood stream!
   Hail, Lord! almighty to create,
   Almighty to redeem.

5. The Mediator's God-like sway
   His church beneath sustains;
   Till Nature shall her Judge survey,
   The King Messiah reigns.

6. Hail, with essential glory crown'd,
   When time shall cease to be,
   Thron'd with thy Father thro' the round
   Of whole eternity.

*Hymn to* GOD *the* HOLY GHOST.

1. Hail, Holy Ghost, Jehovah, third
   In order of the Three;
   Sprung from the Father and the Word
   From all eternity.

2. Thy spirit brooding o'er the abyss
   Of formless waters lay;
   Spoke into order all that is,
   And darkness into day.

3. In deepest hell, or heaven's height,
   Thy presense who can fly?
   Known is the Father to thy sight,
   Th' abyss of Deity.

4. The pow'r thro' Jesu's life display'd
   Quite from the virgin's womb,
   Dying his soul an off'ring made,
   And rais'd him from the tomb.

5. God's image which our sins destroy,
   Thy grace restores below;
   And truth, and holiness, and joy,
   From thee their fountain flow.

6. Hail, Holy Ghost, Jehovah, third
   In order of the Three,
   Spring from the Father and the Word
   From all eternity.

*Hymn to the* TRINITY.

1. Hail, holy, holy, holy Lord!
   Be endless praise to Thee,
   Supreme, essential One, ador'd
   In co-eternal Three:

2. Enthron'd in everlasting state
   Ere time its round began,
   Who join'd in council to create
   The dignity of man.

3. To whom *Isaiah's* vision shew'd
   The seraphs veil their wings,
   While Thee, Jehovah, Lord and God,
   Th' angelic army sings.

4. To Thee by mystic powers on high
   Were humble praises given,
   When *John* beheld with favour'd eye
   Th' inhabitants of heaven.

5. All that the name of creature owns,
   To Thee in hymns aspire:
   May we as angels on our thrones
   For ever join the choir.

6. Hail, holy, holy, holy Lord!
   Be endless praise to Thee,
   Supreme, essential One, ador'd
   In co-eternal Three.

*Another.*

1. Let God the Father live
   For ever on our tongues:
   Sinners from his free love derive
   The ground of all their songs.

2. Ye saints employ your breath
   In honour of the Son,
   Who bought our souls from hell and death
   By off'ring up his own.

C-31

3. Give to the Spirit praise
   Of an immortal strain,
Whole light, and power, and grace conveys
Salvation down to men.

4. While God the Comforter
   Reveals our pardon'd sin,
O may the blood and water bear
   The same record within,

5. To the great One and Three
   That seal the grace in heaven,
The Father, Son, and Spirit, be
   Eternal glory given.

### Another

1. Blest be the Father and his love,
   To whose celestial source we owe
Rivers of endless joy above,
   And rills of comfort here below.

2. Glory to thee, great Son of God;
   Forth from thy wounded body rolls
A precious stream of vital blood,
   Pardon and life for dying souls.

3. We give the sacred Spirit paise,
   Who in our hearts of sin and woe
Makes living springs of grace arise,
   And into boundless glory flow.

4. Thus God the Father, God the Son,
   And God the Spirit we adore;
 · That sea of life, and love unknown,
   Without a bottom or a shore,

### The Divine Perfections.

1. The Lord Jehovah reigns,
   His throne is built on high;
The garments he assumes
   Are light and majesty.
His glories thine with beams so bright,
No mortal eye can bear the sight.

2. The thunders of his hand
   Keep the wide world in awe;
His wrath and justice stand
   To guard his holy law:
And where his love resolves to bless,
His truth confirms and seals the grace.

3. Thro' all his mighty works
   Amazing wisdom shines,
Confounds the powers of hell,
   And breaks their dark designs.
Strong is his arm, and shall fulfil
His great decrees and sovereign will.

4. And can this sovereign King
   Of glory condescend,
And will he write his name,
   My father and my friend!
I love his name, I love his word,
Join all my powers to praise the Lord!

### Sun, Moon; and Stars, Praise ye the LORD.
### Part the First:

1. Regent of all the worlds above,
   Thou sun, whose rays adorn our sphere,
And with unwearied swiftness move
   To form the circle of the year:

2. Praise the Creator of the skies,
   Who decks thy orb with borrow'd rays:
Or may the sun forget to rise,
   When he forgets his Maker's praise.

3. Thou reigning beauty of the night,
   Fair queen of silence, silver moon,
Whose paler fires and female light
   Are softer rivals of the noon:

4. Arise, and to that sovereign power
   Waxing and waning honours pay;
Who bad thee rule the dusky hours,
   And half supply the absent day.

### Part the Second.

1. Ye glitt'ring stars, that gild the skies,
   When darkness has her curtain drawn,
That keep the watch with wakeful eyes,
   When business, cares and day are gone.

2. Proclaim the glories of your Lord,
   Dispers'd through all the heav'nly street,
Whose boundless treasures can afford
   So rich a pavement for his feet.

3. Thou heaven of heavens, supremely bright,
   Fair place of the court divine,
Where with inimitable light
   The Godhead condescends to shine:

4. Praise thou the great inhabitant,
   Who scatters lovely beams of grace
On every angel, every saint,
   Nor veils the lustre of his face.

5. O God of glory, God of love,
   Thou art the sun that mak'st our days:
Midst all thy wondrous works above
   Let earth and dust attempt thy praise.

*Song to* Creating Wisdom.
*Part the First.*

1. Eternal wisdom, thee we praise;
   Thee the creation sings:
   With thy loud name, rocks, hills and seas,
   And heaven's high palace rings.

2. Thy hand how wide it spreads the sky!
   How glorious to behold!
   Ting'd with a blue of heavenly dye,
   And starr'd with sparking gold.

3. There hast thou bid the globes of light
   Their endless circle run:
   There the pale planet rules the night;
   The day obeys the sun.

4. If down I turn, my wandering eyes
   On cloud and storms below,
   Those under-regions of the skies
   Thy num'rous glories show.

5. The noisy winds stand ready there
   Thy order to obey;
   With sounding wings they sweep the air,
   To make thy chariot way.

6. There, like a trumpet loud and strong,
   Thy thunder shakes our coast,
   While the red lightnings wave along
   The banners of thine host.

*Part the Second.*

1. On the thin air without a prop
   Hang fruitful flow'rs around;
   At thy command they sink, and drop
   Their fatness on the ground.

2. Lo here thy wondrous skill arrays
   The fields in cheerful green:
   A thousand herbs thy art displays,
   A thousand flow'res between.

3. There the rough mountains of the deep
   Observe thy strong command;
   Thy breath can raise the billows steep,
   Or sink them to the sand.

4. Thy glories blaze all nature round;
   And strike the wondering sight
   Thro' skies, and seas, and solid ground,
   With terror and delight.

5. Infinite strength and equal skill
   Shine thro' the world abroad,
   Our souls with vast amazement fill,
   And speak the builder God.

6. But the mild glories of thy grace
   Our softer passions move:
   Pity divine in Jesu's face
   We see, adore, and love!

*Thanksgiving for* God*'s particular Providence.*
*Part the first.*

1. When all the mercies of my God
   My rising soul surveys,
   Why, my cold heart, art thou not lost
   In wonder, love, and praise?

2. Thy providence my life sustain'd,
   And all my wants redrest,
   While in the silent womb I lay,
   And hung upon the breast.

3. To all my weak complaints and cries
   Thy mercy lent an ear,
   Ere yet my feeble thoughts had learn'd
   To form themselves in prayer.

4. Unnumber'd comforts on my soul
   Thy tender care bestow'd,
   Before thy infant heart conceiv'd
   From whom those comforts flow'd.

*Part the Second.*

1. When in the slippery paths of youth
   With heedless steps I ran,
   Thine arm unseen convey'd me safe,
   And led me up to man.

2. Thro' hidden dangers, toils, and deaths,
   It gently clear'd my way,
   And thro' the pleasing snares of vice
   More to be fear'd than they.

3. Ten thousand thousand precious gifts
   My daily thanks employ:
   Nor is the least a cheerful heart
   That tastes those gifts with joy.

4. Thro' every period of my life
   Thy goodness I'll pursue;
   And after death in distant worlds
   The pleasing them renew.

C-33

5. Thro' all eternity to thee
    A grateful song I'll raise:
But, O! eternity's too short
    To utter all thy praise.

### GOD *glorious, and Sinners saved.*

1. Father, how wide thy glory shines!
    How high thy wonders rise:
Known, thro' the earth by thousand signs;
    By thousand thro' the skies.

2. Those might orbs proclaim thy power,
    Their motion speak thy skill:
And on the wings of every hour
    We read thy patience still.

3. Part of thy name divinely stands
    On all thy creatures writ;
They shew the labour of thy hands
    Or impress of thy feet.

4. But when we view thy strange design
    To save rebellious worms,
Where vengeance and compassion join
    In their divinest forms:

5. Here the whole Deity is known,
    Nor dares a creature guess,
Which of the glories brightest shone,
    The justice or the grace.

6. Now the full glories of the Lamb
    Adorn the heavenly plains;
Bright seraphs learn *Immanuel's* name,
    And try their choicest strains.

7. O may I hear some humble part
    In that immortal song;
Wonder and joy shall tune my heart,
    And love command my tongue.

### CHRIST *our Wisdom, Righteousness, Sanctification, and Redemption.*

1. Buried in shadows of the night
We lie, 'till Christ restores the light:
Wisdom descends to heal the blind,
And chafe the darkness of the mind.

2. Our guilty souls are drown'd in tears,
Till the atoning blood appears;
Then we awake from deep distress,
And sin the Lord our righteousness.

3. Jesus beholds where Satan reigns
Binding his slaves in heavy chains;
He sets the prisoner free, and breaks
The iron bondage from our necks.

4. Poor helpless worms in thee possess
Grace, wisdom, power, and righteousness:
Thou art our mighty all, and we
Give our whole selves, O Lord, to thee.

### *The Offices of* CHRIST. *Part the First.*

1. Join all the glorious names
    Of wisdom, love, and power,
That ever mortals knew,
    That angels ever bore:
All are too mean to speak thy worth,
Too mean to set thee, *Saviour*, forth.

2. But O what gentle terms,
    What condescending ways
Doth our *Redeemer* use
    To teach his heavenly grace!
Mine eyes with joy and wonder see
What forms of love he bears for me.

3. Array'd in mortal flesh,
    Lo, the *great Angel* stands,
And holds the promises
    And pardons in his hands
Commission'd from his Father's throne,
To make his grace to mortals known.

4. Great *prophet* of my God,
    My tongue shall bless thy name;
By thee the joyfully news
    Of our salvation came,
The joyful news of sins forgiven,
Of hell subdued, and peace with heaven.

5. Be thou my *counselor,*
    My *pattern* and my *guide,*
And thro' this desert land
    Still keep me hear thy side.
O let my feet ne'er run astray,
Nor rove nor seek the crooked way.

6. I love my *shepherd's* voice,
    His watchful eyes shall keep
My wandering soul among
    The thousands of his sheep,
He feeds his flock, he calls their names,
His bosom bears the tender lambs.

### *Part the Second.*

1. Jesus, my great *High-priest,*
    Offer'd his blood and died;
My guilty conscience seeks
    No sacrifice beside.
His pow'rful blood did once atone,
And now it pleads before the throne.

C-34

2. O thou almighty Lord,
   My *Conqueror* and my *King,*
   Thy sceptre and thy sword,
   Thy reigning grace I sing:
Thine is the power, behold I sit
In willing bonds before thy feet.

3. Now let my soul arise,
   And tread the tempter down;
   My *Captain* leads me forth
   To conquest and a crown:
March, on, nor fear to win the day,
Tho' death and hell obstructs the way.

4. Should all the hosts of death,
   And pow'rs of hell unknown,
   Put their most dreadful forms
   Of rage and mischief on;
I shall be safe, for Christ displays
Superior pow'r and guardian grace.

*Triumph over Death.*

1. And must this body die?
   This well-wrought frame decay?
   And must these active limbs of mine
   Lie mouldering in the clay?

2. Corruption, earth, and worms
   Shall but refine this flesh,
   Till my triumphant spirit comes
   To put it on afresh.

3. God my Redeemer lives,
   And ever from the skies
   Looks down, and watches all my dust
   Till he shall bid it rise.

4. Array'd in glorious grace
   Shall these vile bodies shine,
   And every shape and every face
   Be heavenly and divine.

5. These lively hopes we owe,
   Lord, to thy dying love:
   O may we bless thy grace below,
   And sing thy power above.

6. Saviour, accept the praise
   Of these our humble songs,
   Till tunes of nobler sound we raise
   With our immortal tongues.

CHRIST *worshipped by all Creatures:*

1. Come, let us join our cheerful songs
   With angels round the throne;
   Ten thousand thousand are their tongues,
   But all their joys are one.

2. Worthy the Lamb that died, they cry,
   To be exalted thus;
   Worthy the Lamb, our hearts reply,
   For he was slain for us.

3. Jesus is worthy to receive
   Honour and pow'r divine;
   And blessings more than we can give,
   Be, Lord, for ever thine.

4. The whole creation join in one
   To bless the sacred name
   Of him that sits upon the throne,
   And to adore the Lamb.

GOD *our Light in Darkness.*

1. My God, the spring of all my joys,
   The life of my delights,
   The glory of my brightest days,
   And comfort of my nights:

2. In darkest shades, if thou appear
   My dawning is begun:
   Thou art my soul's bright morning-star,
   And thou my rising sun.

3. The opening heavens around me shine
   With beams of sacred bliss,
   If Jesus shews his mercy mine,
   And whispers ''I am his.''

4. My soul would leave this heavy clay
   At that transporting word,
   Run up with joy the shining way,
   To see and praise my Lord.

5. Fearless of hell and ghastly death,
   I'd break thro' every foe:
   The wings of love and arms of faith
   Would bear me conqueror thro'.

*Come,* LORD JESUS!

1. When shall thy lovely face be seen?
   When shall our eyes behold our God?
   What lengths of distance lie between!
   And hills of guilt! A heavy load.

C-35

2. Ye heavenly gates, loose all your chains,
    Let the eternal pillars bow;
 Blest Saviour, cleave the starry plains,
    And make the chrystal mountains flow.

3. Hark! how thy saints unite their cries;
    And pray, and wait the gen'ral doom;
 Come thou! the soul of all our joys;
    Thou, the desire of nations, come!

4. Our heart-strings groan with deep complaint,
    Our flesh lies panting, Lord, for thee;
 And every limb and every joint
    Stretches for immortality.

5. Now let our cheerful eyes survey
    The blazing earth and melting hills;
 And smile to see the lightnings play,
    And flash along before thy wheels.

6. Hark! what a shout of violent joys
    Joins with the might trumpet's sound!
 The angel-herald shakes the skies,
    Awakes the graves, and tears the ground.

7. Ye slumb'ring saints, a heavenly host
    Stands waiting at your gaping tombs;
 Let every sacred, sleeping dust
    Leap into life, for Jesus comes.

8. Jesus, the God of might and love,
    New-moulds our limbs of cumb'rous clay;
 Quick as seraphic flames we move,
    To reign with him in endless days.

# CONTENTS

## PART I.

## PART II.